THE DISCIPLES' PRAYER

A CLOSER LOOK AT MATTHEW 6:9-13

Register This New Book

Benefits of Registering*

- ✓ FREE **replacements** of lost or damaged books
- ✓ FREE **audiobook** – *Pilgrim's Progress*, audiobook edition
- ✓ FREE information about new titles and other **freebies**

www.anekopress.com/new-book-registration

*See our website for requirements and limitations.

greatly encouraged, and my prayer life has become deeper and more focused. I therefore highly commend this book for personal or group study.

Dr. Stephen Gammon
Author, third-generation local church pastor
Conference Minister of Conservative Congregational Christian Conference (2003-2011)
U.S. Navy Chaplain (Retired)
Northfield, Minnesota

In my childhood church, you could set your watch according to the timing of the recitation of the Lord's Prayer. And it was just a recitation. I was in third grade when I first heard my pastor's wife actually *pray* those words with conviction, and I remember thinking, "Are you allowed to do that?"

With this book, from the title to the epilogue, John Kimball exhorts every believer to truly hear the teaching of Jesus and move from babbling recitation to biblical conviction in our prayers. John's balance of clearly explained theology, effective textual examination, and practical application make this book powerfully useful for believers of all physical and spiritual ages.

In order to write this endorsement, I read an advanced electronic version of *The Disciples' Prayer*. I cannot wait to get a hard copy so that I can highlight and underline and wrestle with the *Aha*s that are contained on nearly every page. I look forward to working through the "Putting It into Practice" questions as I seek to employ this kingdom-prayer framework for the advance of His kingdom and His glory. I cannot recommend this book highly enough!

Susan E. Moody
Pastor, Transitional/Intentional Interim Ministry
Summerfield, Florida

Dr. Kimball writes a masterful book on prayer that moves the reader from a simple conceptual understanding of the Disciples' Prayer to a practice that can be engaged daily to enhance our relationship with the Father and assist in overcoming the problem of prayerlessness in the lives of so many. This is a wonderful book for the new believer, the disciple that is seeking to grow in prayer, and the saint that longs for more in their relationship with Christ. To quote Dr. Kimball, this prayer is a "Kingdom prayer by Kingdom citizens exercising Kingdom authority for God's Kingdom mission." I encourage you to read and invite people to read it with you.

Mike Chong Perkinson
Superintendent of the PCJC Network of the Free Methodist Church, USA
Cofounder and Senior Developer of The Praxis Center for Church Development
President and Dean of Church & Ministry at Trivium Institute of Leader Development
Lake Elsinore, California

As I began to read John Kimball's book *The Disciples' Prayer,* I was captured immediately by how he brought such intimacy to the One to whom our prayer is directed, our Father. I could have stopped there, and the book would have been worth the read. John, through his writing, created a desire in my heart to celebrate this intimacy with the Father by illustrating the significance of His being our provider, our protector, and the very source of our identity. Living out of this intimacy is certainly a way of life for the Christ-follower.

John goes on to elaborate on the definition and realities of the kingdom of God, human needs, as well as protection from the Evil One.

This is more than a book about prayer – it is a call to a deeper relationship with our Father, a reminder of His kingdom purposes, and an encouragement to align our hearts with His will. It challenged me to a more full, personal, and intimate prayer life.

Dr. T. A. Powell
Instructor, Rawlings School of Divinity, Liberty University
Adjunct Professor of Divinity, Regent University
Smithfield, Virginia

With rich theological insights and thoughtful questions, this book deepens our prayer life and embraces all that this prayer has to offer us as we live in the now-but-not-yet kingdom. This book is designed for those seeking greater intimacy with Abba, God our Father.

Dr. Amy Bragg Carey
President, Friends University
Wichita, Kansas

Few books on the Lord's Prayer demonstrate the depth and clarity found in John Kimball's remarkable work. Unlike many others, Kimball masterfully weaves together the chronology of Jesus' ministry, the profound Christology of His person, and the urgent priority of His mission. Years of thoughtful reflection, rigorous research, and practical insight into what he calls the Disciple's Prayer – encompassing scriptural truths about Jesus' character and priorities, historical insights from the first-century world, and practical applications for today – have culminated in this empowering resource. I enthusiastically commend this book to anyone intent on living out the reality of Jesus' kingdom prayer and kingdom mission in the now, even while we await the eventual ultimate kingdom yet to come.

Dr. Jim Culbertson
President, New England Bible College & Seminary
Global Movement Catalyst, Concentric Global
Disciple-Making
Augusta, Maine

In this excellent book, *The Disciples' Prayer*, John Kimball offers profound and perceptive teaching on what is commonly called the Lord's Prayer. He also beautifully guides the reader to put it all into practice by being real and honest in prayerful reflection, seeking and listening carefully to God, and thus growing closer in true intimacy with Him. After each section of insightful biblical teaching on praying as Jesus taught us, there are helpful questions for personal reflection or group discussion to assist readers in understanding and applying to their daily lives how our Lord is inviting His disciples to live and pray. By prayerfully reading this book, my own faith was stretched, my heart was

In this powerful book, Pastor John gives new life to the Lord's Prayer, transforming what can often become a rote recitation into a meaningful conversation with God. By breaking it down line by line, he reveals the depth of Jesus' intention, making it understandable and applicable to our daily lives. This book is a valuable resource for those who truly want to pray as Jesus taught us, with purpose and passion.

Toni McAndrew
Missionary to the Deaf and Hard of Hearing, Latin America Mission (Retired)
TBLESSA (Sign Language) Bible Translation Team, Wycliffe Bible Translators
San Salvador, El Salvador/Virginia Beach, VA

The Disciples' Prayer is a courageous and refreshing call to rediscover the power of prayer as Jesus intended it. John Kimball masterfully bridges Scripture and everyday life, showing how prayer is not a ritual but a kingdom reality that transforms us from within. His approach is radical in its depth, balanced in its theology, passionate in tone, and thoroughly researched. This book will not only teach you how to pray but will also inspire you to live as one whose life is continually shaped by the presence and authority of God.

Dr. Petr Činčala
Associate Professor of Missions and Research
Director of the Institute of Church Ministry and DIS program, Andrews University
U.S. National Partner for Natural Church Development
Berrien Springs, MI

Every Christ-follower intuitively knows they should pray, but how? The question started some two thousand years ago with Jesus' own apprentices. In response, Jesus provided them with a comprehensive blueprint for prayer. Pastor John's excellent book helps put the master plan of prayer together. Read it and you will grow in your capacity to lovingly converse with our Abba Father.

Marc S. Gauthier
Conference Minister, Conservative Congregational Christian Conference
Lake Elmo, Minnesota

THE DISCIPLES' PRAYER

The Simple Yet Profound Framework Jesus Gave His Followers to Use in Prayer

JOHN KIMBALL

The Disciples' Prayer

© 2025 by John R. Kimball

All rights reserved. Published 2025.

Please do not reproduce, store in a retrieval system, or transmit in any form or by any means – electronic, mechanical, photocopying, recording, or otherwise, without written permission from the publisher.

Scripture quotations are from the ESV® Bible (The Holy Bible, English Standard Version®), © 2001 by Crossway, a publishing ministry of Good News Publishers. ESV Text Edition: 2025. The ESV text may not be quoted in any publication made available to the public by a Creative Commons license. The ESV may not be translated in whole or in part into any other language. Used by permission. All rights reserved.

Cover Designer: J. Martin

Praying hands on cover: takahuli.production/Shutterstock

Underline graphic: sumkinn/Shutterstock

Editor: Paul Miller

Aneko Press

www.anekopress.com

inquiries@anekopress.com

Aneko Press, Life Sentence Publishing, and our logos are trademarks of

Life Sentence Publishing, Inc.
203 E. Birch Street
P.O. Box 652
Abbotsford, WI 54405

RELIGION / Christian Living / Prayer

Paperback ISBN: 978-1-62245-617-8

eBook ISBN: 978-1-62245-618-5

10 9 8 7 6 5 4 3 2 1

Available where books are sold

To my dear friend and mentor, Tom Johnston, who has invested deeply in my life and ministry for several years and who helped me become an authentic disciple of Jesus.

Converts are *convinced* of something.
Believers *believe* something.
Disciples *become* like the rabbi.

Contents

Acknowledgments xiii
The Lord's Prayer xv
Preface xvii
Introduction: The Disciples' Prayer xxi

Part One: The One to Whom We Pray 1
   1. Our Father 3
   2. In the Heavens 23

Part Two: Kingdom Realities Today 35
   3. Be Holy, Your Name! 37
   4. Come, Your Kingdom! 53
   5. Be Done, Your Will! 65

Part Three: Human Needs Covered 77
   6. Give Us Tomorrow's Bread Today 79
   7. Forgive Us As We Forgive Others 91
   8. Protect Us from Evil 103

Epilogue: Praying with Kingdom Power 121

Appendixes 125
   1. The Shema 127
   2. The Kiddush 131
   3. The Amidah 133

About the Author 143

Acknowledgments

This book took my entire adult life and ministerial career to write. As such, there is no way I can adequately thank all of the wonderful people who played a role in its creation. There are entire congregations around the country that have been part of this many-year journey as I taught and preached on prayer in their churches. While many people have been part of this book's meandering path to publication, there are a few for whom I must express special gratitude.

I must first thank my bride, Kathryn, for being my biggest cheerleader on this project. She was the first to suggest (in 1992) that it needed to be put into a book, and she reminded me of this many times during the ensuing thirty-three years. I would also like to thank my daughter Lauren for two early content suggestions that turned out to be vital to the ideas I was trying to convey.

I would like to thank my dear friend and mentor, Tom Johnston, for his support. As we discussed the writing of this book, he suggested that I not write it "devotionally," but that I pay attention to what Jesus was actually instructing His disciples to do in the prayer. He pointed to a few key things that, with much additional study, launched me in an entirely different direction. The book you have in your hand would not be the same (nor would my prayer life be the same) without that Zoom call.

I would like to thank my national Nehemiah Nexus Church Development Team for their support and input, and particularly Peter Wood and Ed Enstine for introducing me to the works of Joachim Jeremias. His seminal work on Jesus' prayer life played a significant role in my own understanding of the incredible prayer framework Jesus taught His beloved disciples.

Finally, I would love to thank Jon Rismiller, Scott Littlefield, Jim Bertoti, and Steve Gammon for reading my text and providing encouragement, critical perspective, and theological clarity. Steve Gammon also provided important publishing guidance. Thanks also to several others who read each chapter and gave me feedback on making a deeply theological work as user-friendly as possible.

To my Abba be the glory,
John Kimball

The Lord's Prayer

Our Father in heaven,
hallowed be your name.
Your kingdom come,
your will be done,
on earth as it is in heaven.
Give us this day our daily bread,
and forgive us our debts,
as we also have forgiven our debtors.
And lead us not into temptation,
but deliver us from evil.
—Matthew 6:9-13

Preface

When I began my first senior pastorate in May 1992, I started with a sermon series on the Lord's Prayer. I told my new congregation that if I had only one opportunity to influence a church family for Jesus' kingdom, I would want to teach them to pray. If we have a robust prayer life, it influences everything else. That deliberate "unpacking" of Jesus' lesson on prayer became a spiritual marker for me and many others.

Over the many years of local and national ministry, I have had many opportunities to teach this lesson. Each time, I have discovered more of the richness provided in our Savior's prayer framework. I have also been encouraged more than once to write a book on the topic.

After a powerful personal encounter with the Lord, I finally set out to write *The Disciples' Prayer* in October 2024. I sensed explicit instruction from Him that the time had come. Over the next few months, however, I was surprised at how much I would add to my understanding of this model prayer. My friend and mentor,

Dr. Tom Johnston, commented during a Zoom meeting about how Jesus plays with time and space in the prayer. I had not noticed that before. I expanded my study and did more serious work, analyzing the Greek phrasing used in the prayer. I reread George Eldon Ladd's *The Gospel of the Kingdom* (something I do every few years) and was profoundly moved by how the prayer lined up with Ladd's "now, but not yet" motif on the kingdom of God. I discovered a teaching series by John Wimber on the Lord's Prayer that provided many critical insights. Some friends also encouraged me to read the work of Joachim Jeremias entitled *The Prayers of Jesus*. Suddenly, my perspective on Jesus' prayer outline changed significantly. What is more, my own prayer life deepened dramatically.

My prayer is that this book will forever change your prayer life as it expands your understanding of the simple yet profound framework Jesus gave His followers to use in prayer. The book is divided into three essential parts, following Jesus' outline in the gospel of Matthew. After a brief introduction, we study:

1. Approaching the Person to Whom We Pray

2. Calling Specific Kingdom Realities into Being

3. Asking for Critical Personal Needs to Be Met

All of these are set within our intimate relationship with God in Jesus Christ and are designed to enable us to live here on earth as victorious and fruitful citizens of God's kingdom.

May the Holy Spirit use your time in this text for

His purposes and God's glory. May you never see the Lord's Prayer the same again. And may you discover a new level of richness in both your prayer life and your walk with Jesus. This has certainly been true for me.

John Kimball
Oviedo, Florida
June 2025

Introduction

The Disciples' Prayer

First, Thy name, Thy kingdom, Thy will;
then, give us, forgive us, lead us, deliver us.
The lesson is of more importance than we
think. In true worship the Father must be
first, must be all.
—Andrew Murray, in *Lord, Teach Us to Pray*

The Dilemma

Do you pray? In what way? Do you lift up urgent requests? Do you have a consistent, ongoing conversation with God throughout each day? Do you intercede daily for your neighborhood? For your city? For your world? Do you pray for God's rule and reign to cover humanity? Are you genuinely thankful, expressing gratitude to God for all His blessings? Do you pray for your own provision? For protection? Who taught you to pray? Are you seeing regular answers to your prayers?

One of the most significant impediments to life and

ministry in the modern church of the West today is the lack of prayer. Christians simply do not pray as they should. Prayer is a last hope for most people instead of the first and persistent expression of our faith in Christ. And while recent studies show a growing desire for prayer across many generations, the practice of prayer tends to be more self-centered and in response to perceived stress and crises. In my work with congregations across America, I have noticed not only a lack of the robust prayer described in the Scriptures, but also a near-complete deficit in teaching on prayer. I wonder if people are not earnest in prayer because we have not helped them understand and experience both the powerful divine purpose and the process of praying. We lack much of God's intended power and fruit today because we are not spending adequate time with the Father; what's worse, our motivations are often skewed (James 4:2-3). Then we must add another problem layer: we have an enemy who knows what will happen if God's people begin to pray rightly. He masterfully distracts people from regularly entering into prayer conversations with our heavenly Father.

Prayer is powerful. When the Christian prays, he or she prays with the authority of the King of all kings and the Lord of all lords. Jesus commissions His followers (Matthew 28:18-20), and we are, therefore, His authorized ambassadors (2 Corinthians 5:20). Prayer was a nonnegotiable aspect of Jesus' life (Luke 5:16). If we are called to become like Jesus, then prayer must be a consistent nonnegotiable aspect of our lives as well.

Thankfully, Jesus taught His disciples *how* to pray.

THE DISCIPLES' PRAYER

And when you pray, you must not be like the hypocrites. For they love to stand and pray in the synagogues and at the street corners, that they may be seen by others. Truly, I say to you, they have received their reward. But when you pray, go into your room and shut the door and pray to your Father who is in secret. And your Father who sees in secret will reward you.

And when you pray, do not heap up empty phrases as the Gentiles do, for they think that they will be heard for their many words. Do not be like them, for your Father knows what you need before you ask him. Pray then like this:

Our Father in heaven,
hallowed be your name.
Your kingdom come,
your will be done,
on earth as it is in heaven.
Give us this day our daily bread,
and forgive us our debts,
as we also have forgiven our debtors.
And lead us not into temptation,
but deliver us from evil.

For if you forgive others their trespasses, your heavenly Father will also forgive you, but if you do not forgive others their trespasses, neither will your Father forgive your trespasses. (Matthew 6:5-15)

The Lesson and the Kingdom

Jesus provided His lesson on prayer in response to a request from one of His disciples: *Lord, teach us to pray, as John taught his disciples* (Luke 11:1). In Jesus' day, rabbis typically provided a framework for prayer consistent with their *yoke* – their particular lineage of teaching and practice of the Torah (the Law of Moses) as handed down from great rabbis of the past. But Jesus had His own yoke. That is what He was referring to when He said:

> *Come to me, all who labor and are heavy laden, and I will give you rest. Take my yoke upon you, and learn from me, for I am gentle and lowly in heart, and you will find rest for your souls. For my yoke is easy, and my burden is light.* (Matthew 11:28-30)

Jesus spoke and taught on His own authority, not on that of other rabbis. He would then demonstrate the veracity of His yoke's authority through miracles (Matthew 7:28-29; Mark 1:21-28). His authority was tested (Matthew 21:23-27), but the religious leaders could not find fault with either Him or His teaching (John 3:2).

Jesus' rabbinical yoke centered on the kingdom of God. There is nothing more important than the King and his kingdom.[1] The prayer Jesus taught was a kingdom prayer. The disciples had seen Jesus' practice of

---

1   Tom Johnston, Mike Chong Perkinson, Deryk Richenburg, and Tim McGinnin, *Alignment Participant's Workbook: A Discipleship Process* (Bedford, NH: Praxis Media, 2024), 15.

prayer and solitude over time. They had seen its results and they wanted to pray as their rabbi prayed. The unnamed disciple's request acknowledges that other rabbis, including John the Baptist, had provided their *talmidim* (disciples, students) with prayer frameworks based on their yokes. Jesus responded by giving His own prayer framework, rooted in His authoritative teaching of the kingdom of God. We traditionally call it "The Lord's Prayer" (more on that in a bit).

The Kingdom of God Is Now, But Not Yet

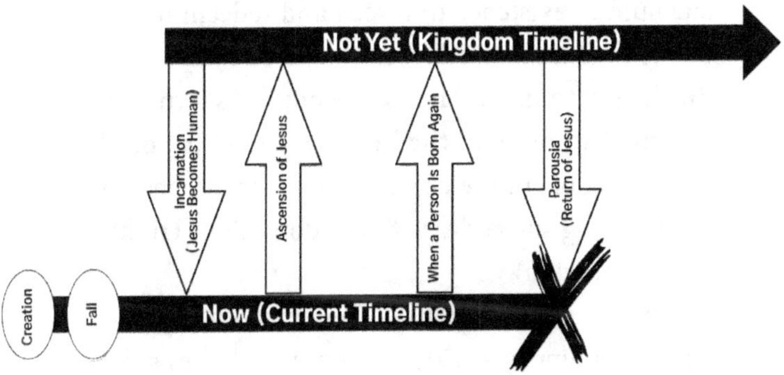

A diagram showing two parallel timeline arrows. The top arrow is labeled "Not Yet (Kingdom Timeline)" and the bottom arrow is labeled "Now (Current Timeline)". On the bottom timeline, from left to right: "Creation", "Fall", and an X marking the end. Arrows connect between the two timelines at four points labeled: "Incarnation (Jesus Becomes Human)", "Ascension of Jesus", "When a Person Is Born Again", and "Parousia (Return of Jesus)".

The kingdom aspect of Jesus' prayer cannot be ignored. George Eldon Ladd has beautifully explained the unique state of the kingdom of God today as "now, but not yet."[2] The kingdom of God among fallen humanity began when Jesus became human ("now"), but will not be fully established until Jesus returns in power and glory ("not yet"). In this prayer, Jesus is teaching

---

2   George Eldon Ladd, *The Gospel of the Kingdom: Scriptural Studies in the Kingdom of God* (Grand Rapids: Paternoster Press, 1959). I highly recommend this book as supplemental reading to any study of the Lord's Prayer.

His disciples to exercise kingdom authority – literally calling the realities of the coming kingdom of God into the "now" where they currently live.

Ladd shows us that between Jesus' incarnation (becoming human) and His parousia (second coming), there are two concurrent timelines. This is still true for us today. There is the current timeline, or the "now" into which we are born, that is corrupted by sin and has all of creation under Satan's dominion of darkness,[3] and there is the kingdom timeline that was ushered in as King Jesus was incarnate and entered into our human existence to rescue and redeem us. Jesus was *of* the kingdom timeline, but lived *in* the current timeline with us. At His ascension, Jesus returned to His rightful place in the kingdom timeline, but left behind people in the current timeline who belong to Him, having surrendered to His dominion (His kingship, rule, reign).

They are now citizens of the kingdom (Ephesians 2:18-22; Philippians 3:20-21), even though they still live on this earth. Each of us enters the kingdom timeline when we are born again. This is what Jesus meant when He referred to us as being *in* the world but not *of* the world (John 17:11-19). This is why we cannot serve both God and earthly riches as our master (Matthew 6:24).

We will see that Jesus' rabbinical prayer framework authorizes us to call several realities of the kingdom of God into our *now*. This is the very essence of Jesus'

---

[3] See John Kimball, *Low-Hanging Fruit: Partnering with the Holy Spirit for Greater Ministry Impact* (Oviedo, FL: The Beaumeadow Group, 2022), 10-11, for my explanation of Satan's usurped authority and subsequent dark dominion over creation.

words: *on earth as it is in heaven*. As my adaptation of Ladd's diagram (above) shows, the current timeline will come to an end when King Jesus returns in power and glory.[4] After that, only God's kingdom will go on (with us in it) for all eternity.

Two Admonitions

I find it fascinating that Jesus started His prayer lesson by teaching His disciples how *not* to pray. He gives us two admonitions: The first is to avoid showy, hypocritical praying (Matthew 6:5-6), and the second is to avoid empty, babbly praying (Matthew 6:7-8). Neither of these provides a legitimate avenue of communication with our loving heavenly Father, nor do they invoke the pertinent realities of His kingdom rule and reign. Hypocritical praying is self-centered. Empty praying is useless.

In many churches today, the Lord's Prayer is recited every Sunday during worship. There is nothing wrong with repeating the prayer, but in too many cases, people mindlessly drone on in "autopilot" mode without thinking. Ironically, some people "babble" the very prayer taught to help us avoid empty, babbly praying! God's precious children must be engaged, intentional, and consistent in praying this powerful kingdom prayer.

The Father's Response

Jesus' prayer lesson is found in two primary passages: Matthew 6:5-15 and Luke 11:1-13. They are given at two

---

4 Ladd, *Gospel*, 42.

different times to two different audiences, so it's important to study them both. In Luke's account, Jesus concludes His teaching by describing God's loving response to our prayers:

> *And he said to them, "Which of you who has a friend will go to him at midnight and say to him, 'Friend, lend me three loaves, for a friend of mine has arrived on a journey, and I have nothing to set before him'; and he will answer from within, 'Do not bother me; the door is now shut, and my children are with me in bed. I cannot get up and give you anything'? I tell you, though he will not get up and give him anything because he is his friend, yet because of his impudence he will rise and give him whatever he needs. And I tell you, ask, and it will be given to you; seek, and you will find; knock, and it will be opened to you. For everyone who asks receives, and the one who seeks finds, and to the one who knocks it will be opened. What father among you, if his son asks for a fish, will instead of a fish give him a serpent; or if he asks for an egg, will give him a scorpion? If you then, who are evil, know how to give good gifts to your children, how much more will the heavenly Father give the Holy Spirit to those who ask him!"* (Luke 11:5-13)

Jesus' rabbinical question uses absurdity to elicit a response. He is not saying that God is like the grumpy friend. His point is that if even sinful human beings can act correctly, how much more will our loving heavenly Father provide for us out of His infinite goodness? Jesus also shows us that God desires persistence in our praying. Persistence is critical. Jesus' explanation is filled with continuous action verbs: ask is "ask and keep on asking"; seek is "seek and keep on seeking"; and knock is "knock and keep on knocking."

The Father responds with love and kingdom abundance to our persistent prayers. His greatest gift is the Holy Spirit. The Holy Spirit is our source of spiritual life and fruit (John 6:63; Galatians 5:22-23). The Holy Spirit guides us in our praying (Romans 8:26-27). The Holy Spirit leads us into all truth (John 16:13). When we pray fervently, persistently, and in the way Jesus taught us, the Father lavishes all these things upon us.

Looking Ahead

This prayer is a kingdom prayer by kingdom citizens exercising kingdom authority for God's kingdom mission. This book was written to guide you into the beautiful depths of Jesus' prayer lesson. Much of it is very straightforward and practical, but some things we review together may be surprisingly new and deep. All of it is to help us spend precious and powerful time with our heavenly Father. If we want to learn to pray like Jesus, then we need to spend time engaging with and implementing Jesus' lesson on prayer!

I've chosen not to call this book *The Lord's Prayer*. I have always considered Jesus' high priestly prayer in John 17 the *Lord's* prayer for us. The prayer we're unpacking in this book is really the *disciples'* prayer. It is Jesus' lesson – His powerful framework – given to His disciples as they begged Jesus to teach them to pray like He prayed. And while we are not among the original twelve disciples, Ladd shows us that all those who surrender to Jesus as King and accept His commission to complete His mission are indeed kingdom citizens along with His disciples. Jesus had hundreds (if not thousands) of disciples by the time He ascended, and you and I are counted among that growing number if we belong to Him today. This is *our* prayer.

Part One

The One to Whom We Pray

> Most Christians do not have fellowship with God. They have fellowship with each other about God.
>
> —Paris Reidhead

After explaining that our praying should never be for hypocritical self-aggrandizement like the Pharisees of His day prayed (Matthew 6:5-6), nor should it be mindless babbling like the pagans displayed (Matthew 6:7-8), Jesus gives the first of many imperatives regarding our prayer: *Pray then like this* . . . It is given with the force of a command. He then leads His disciples (then and now) into a clear understanding of the One to whom we pray so that we pray with the right attitude, perspective, and posture.

Chapter 1

Our Father

Our Father in heaven, hallowed be your name. (Matthew 6:9)

It is through the work of Christ that God invites us to call him "Abba, Father." It is through Christ that grace and peace have resulted, and we have become God's children.

—Walter A. Elwell

The Intimacy of "Abba"

To the Jews of Jesus' day, God was almighty, transcendent, and holy. The understanding of God as "Father" was reserved for Israel as a people (see Exodus 4:22-23; Psalm 103:13; Isaiah 63:16-17). Before Jesus' earthly ministry, aside from notable exceptions such as King David, the idea that God is intimate was simply not the norm. Even to this day, the name of God is too holy for Jews to speak. When referring to God, the vowels are removed to make the actual word unpronounceable (e.g., "G-d"). One would not address God in prayer using familiar terms; it just was not done.

When Jesus referred to God by the Aramaic term *Abba* ("Daddy" or "Papa"), it was revolutionary. God is not a distant God, but rather one who is *with* us. God is an intimate God. And while Jesus' lesson on prayer is transmitted to us using the more formal Greek word *Pater* ("Father"), Jesus would have taught this prayer lesson to His disciples in their native Aramaic. Further, He proclaimed God as *our* Father. Jesus' relationship with the Father is different from ours. He is God's only *begotten* son (John 3:16) – Jesus alone has God's divine nature. But those who surrender to Jesus' lordship are children by adoption. We are given full rights as God's sons and daughters (John 1:12-13). Therefore, Jesus makes it clear that His followers also call God "Abba" (John 20:17).

Talking about the first line of the disciples' prayer, James Bryan Smith explains the intimacy with which he prays to the Father – praying to God as "Dearest Abba" and "The One to Whom I belong."[5] Something changes when we pray with such intimacy. Jesus teaches us not to just pray to *the* Father, but to *our* Father. Jesus teaches those who follow Him, redeemed by His blood, to call God "Abba." Paul continues that thought in his letters:

---

5   James Bryan Smith, host, *Things Above Podcast*, episode 30, "Talk to God," Apple Podcasts, October 2, 2024, https://apprenticeinstitute.org/2024/10/02/talk-to-god/.

*For all who are led by the Spirit of God
are sons of God. For you did not receive
the spirit of slavery to fall back into fear,
but you have received the Spirit of adoption as sons, by whom we cry, "Abba!
Father!" The Spirit himself bears witness
with our spirit that we are children of God.*
(Romans 8:14-16)

*But when the fullness of time had come,
God sent forth his Son, born of woman,
born under the law, to redeem those who
were under the law, so that we might receive
adoption as sons. And because you are sons,
God has sent the Spirit of his Son into our
hearts, crying, "Abba! Father!" So you are
no longer a slave, but a son, and if a son,
then an heir through God.* (Galatians 4:4-7)

Paul's usage of "Abba" in these ways presupposes that Jesus frequently used "Abba" as a form to address God.[6] If we are in Christ, we are God's precious, beloved, redeemed daughters and sons. While there can and should be a measure of reverence and awe in approaching our Abba, our Father, there is no longer any need for terror before Him, because that kind of fear is rooted in a broken relationship with God that is destined for judgment. That is no longer our destiny!

John writes:

---

6 Joachim Jeremias, *The Prayers of Jesus* (Philadelphia: Fortress Press, 1967), 55.

> *Whoever confesses that Jesus is the Son of God, God abides in him, and he in God. So we have come to know and to believe the love that God has for us. God is love, and whoever abides in love abides in God, and God abides in him. By this is love perfected with us, so that we may have confidence for the day of judgment, because as he is so also are we in this world. There is no fear in love, but perfect love casts out fear. For fear has to do with punishment, and whoever fears has not been perfected in love. We love because he first loved us.* (1 John 4:15-19)

God, our Father, *abides* in us, and we in Him! We do not pray in fear to a distant God. We converse with our heavenly Abba, who loves us, has redeemed us, and has removed the judgment of sin from us by the already shed blood of Jesus. We pray with intimacy. We pray in infinite love. And this is where Jesus instructs us to begin.

It's Not Just a Title

When Jesus instructs His followers to call God Almighty "Our Father," it's not just a title. It's not a role He plays. To the first-century Jew, "father" meant something. And as Jesus and His apostles flesh out our relationship with our heavenly Father, that meaning grows deep and beautiful. We will concentrate on three key aspects of our Abba's fatherhood related to prayer.

Jewish culture has great respect for family elders,

and in Jesus' day, many Jewish extended families lived together in ever-expanding family compounds called *insulas*. Each generation would build onto the compound, with a central courtyard for whole-family gatherings, meals, teaching, worship, and other events. Fathers and grandfathers played a crucial role in this family life. Beyond leading the family, the father of the household was the provider, often the primary overseer of the family trade. The father was also the protector of the family. The father passed the family name and identity on to the following generations. The father was the authority in the family, and they trusted his leadership. When Jesus taught His followers to address the Ancient of Days as "Our Father," they would have associated God with all these characteristics and more. Jesus' use of "Abba" in His own prayers is an expression of obedient trust and a recognition of God's authority.[7]

Abba: Our Provider

When we pray to our Abba as our Father, we stop and recognize that He is our provider. So many Christians are consumed with various aspects of provision in their lives. Much anxiety comes from worrying about personal finances, careers, housing, and adequate medical care. To pray to God as our loving, intimate, heavenly Father is to surrender to the fact that He will care for us.

Jesus expressed this very practically in the verses that follow His teaching on prayer in Matthew's gospel:

---

[7] Jeremias, *Prayers*, 63.

Therefore I tell you, do not be anxious about your life, what you will eat or what you will drink, nor about your body, what you will put on. Is not life more than food, and the body more than clothing? Look at the birds of the air: they neither sow nor reap nor gather into barns, and yet your heavenly Father feeds them. Are you not of more value than they? And which of you by being anxious can add a single hour to his span of life? And why are you anxious about clothing? Consider the lilies of the field, how they grow: they neither toil nor spin, yet I tell you, even Solomon in all his glory was not arrayed like one of these. But if God so clothes the grass of the field, which today is alive and tomorrow is thrown into the oven, will he not much more clothe you, O you of little faith? Therefore do not be anxious, saying, "What shall we eat?" or "What shall we drink?" or "What shall we wear?" For the Gentiles seek after all these things, and your heavenly Father knows that you need them all. But seek first the kingdom of God and his righteousness, and all these things will be added to you.

Therefore do not be anxious about tomorrow, for tomorrow will be anxious for itself. Sufficient for the day is its own trouble. (Matthew 6:25-34)

Jesus tells His followers to trust in God's provision. We are not to be anxious about our lives, food, bodies, and clothing – because He takes care of the rest of creation, and we are far more valuable to Him than birds and flowers. Jesus drives the point home by asking, *And which of you by being anxious can add a single hour to his span of life?* In fact, modern medicine shows us that such anxiety actually does the opposite!

We must learn to trust God and His loving provision. He knows our needs better than we know them ourselves. He has everything we will ever need at His disposal. He loves us deeply. Every time we pray "Our Father," we surrender to His love and provision.

Abba: Our Protector

In addition to being our provider, our Abba is also our protector. He is not just our protector in times of danger, but at all times and in all areas of life. While we're not sure who penned it (many attribute it to Moses), the author of Psalm 91 uniquely understood this.

> *He who dwells in the shelter of the Most High*
> *will abide in the shadow of the Almighty.*
> *I will say to the L*ORD*, "My refuge and my fortress,*
> *my God, in whom I trust."*
> *For he will deliver you from the snare of the fowler*
> *and from the deadly pestilence.*
> *He will cover you with his pinions,*
> *and under his wings you will find refuge;*
> *his faithfulness is a shield and buckler.*

You will not fear the terror of the night,
nor the arrow that flies by day,
nor the pestilence that stalks in darkness,
nor the destruction that wastes at noonday.
A thousand may fall at your side,
ten thousand at your right hand,
but it will not come near you.
You will only look with your eyes
and see the recompense of the wicked.
Because you have made the LORD your dwelling place—
the Most High, who is my refuge—
no evil shall be allowed to befall you,
no plague come near your tent.
For he will command his angels concerning you
to guard you in all your ways.
On their hands they will bear you up,
lest you strike your foot against a stone.
You will tread on the lion and the adder;
the young lion and the serpent you will trample underfoot.
"Because he holds fast to me in love, I will deliver him;
I will protect him, because he knows my name.
When he calls to me, I will answer him;
I will be with him in trouble;
I will rescue him and honor him.
With long life I will satisfy him
and show him my salvation." (Psalm 91:1-16)

I particularly love the psalmist's words, *He will cover you with his pinions, and under his wings you will find refuge.* The picture is of a mother bird pulling her wing over her chicks to cover and protect them. There is a similar picture painted in Deuteronomy 32:11-12. Many Bible passages attribute this picture of maternal love and protection to God. The prophet Isaiah uses this imagery multiple times to describe God's love for His people. The prophet Hosea has a slightly different take, describing God as a mother bear who has been robbed of her cubs (Hosea 13:8). The image of a mother bird gathering her young may also be seen in Jesus' heart as He laments over Jerusalem (Matthew 23:37; Luke 13:34-35). However, the most powerful demonstration of this covering love is seen in Exodus 12:

> *The LORD said to Moses and Aaron in the land of Egypt, "This month shall be for you the beginning of months. It shall be the first month of the year for you. Tell all the congregation of Israel that on the tenth day of this month every man shall take a lamb according to their fathers' houses, a lamb for a household. And if the household is too small for a lamb, then he and his nearest neighbor shall take according to the number of persons; according to what each can eat you shall make your count for the lamb. Your lamb shall be without blemish, a male a year old. You may take it from the sheep or from the goats, and you shall keep it until the*

fourteenth day of this month, when the whole assembly of the congregation of Israel shall kill their lambs at twilight.

"Then they shall take some of the blood and put it on the two doorposts and the lintel of the houses in which they eat it. They shall eat the flesh that night, roasted on the fire; with unleavened bread and bitter herbs they shall eat it. Do not eat any of it raw or boiled in water, but roasted, its head with its legs and its inner parts. And you shall let none of it remain until the morning; anything that remains until the morning you shall burn. In this manner you shall eat it: with your belt fastened, your sandals on your feet, and your staff in your hand. And you shall eat it in haste. It is the Lord's Passover. For I will pass through the land of Egypt that night, and I will strike all the firstborn in the land of Egypt, both man and beast; and on all the gods of Egypt I will execute judgments: I am the Lord. The blood shall be a sign for you, on the houses where you are. And when I see the blood, I will pass over you, and no plague will befall you to destroy you, when I strike the land of Egypt.

"This day shall be for you a memorial day, and you shall keep it as a feast to the Lord; throughout your generations, as a statute

forever, you shall keep it as a feast. Seven days you shall eat unleavened bread. On the first day you shall remove leaven out of your houses, for if anyone eats what is leavened, from the first day until the seventh day, that person shall be cut off from Israel. On the first day you shall hold a holy assembly, and on the seventh day a holy assembly. No work shall be done on those days. But what everyone needs to eat, that alone may be prepared by you. And you shall observe the Feast of Unleavened Bread, for on this very day I brought your hosts out of the land of Egypt. Therefore you shall observe this day, throughout your generations, as a statute forever. In the first month, from the fourteenth day of the month at evening, you shall eat unleavened bread until the twenty-first day of the month at evening. For seven days no leaven is to be found in your houses. If anyone eats what is leavened, that person will be cut off from the congregation of Israel, whether he is a sojourner or a native of the land. You shall eat nothing leavened; in all your dwelling places you shall eat unleavened bread."

Then Moses called all the elders of Israel and said to them, "Go and select lambs for yourselves according to your clans, and kill the Passover lamb. Take a bunch of hyssop and dip it in the blood that is in the basin,

> *and touch the lintel and the two doorposts with the blood that is in the basin. None of you shall go out of the door of his house until the morning. For the LORD will pass through to strike the Egyptians, and when he sees the blood on the lintel and on the two doorposts, the LORD will pass over the door and will not allow the destroyer to enter your houses to strike you.* (Exodus 12:1-23)

As God tells the Hebrews, *I will pass over you*, He expresses His protection over His people. Some people think of the words "pass over you" as skipping the houses with lamb's blood on the doorposts and lintels of the doors. But a better translation in these verses might be "hover over you," "shelter you," or "cover you" in protection (Exodus 12:23, 27; Isaiah 31:5). Especially as seen in Exodus 12:23, the Lord is *covering* and *protecting* the Hebrew homes that have blood on their doors, not allowing death to touch those households.

Our Abba, God, our heavenly Father, is our ultimate protector. When we pray "Our Father," we recognize His loving and thorough protection over us.

Abba: The Source of Our Identity

A person's identity tells us the most important thing about themselves. In the United States, our culture leads us to find our identity in what we do for a living or in our role. When we greet someone for the first time, we immediately ask, "What do you do?" That is how we identify a person: "I'm a butcher." "I'm a baker." "I'm a candlestick maker." "I'm a mom." Beyond that, some people find their identity in their ethnicity. Others find their identity in their community, their denominational label, their culture, their hobbies, or their gender. Some even find their identity in an illness or another cause of suffering. However, for the follower of Jesus, one must find his or her identity primarily in being a precious, beloved, redeemed child of our Abba in Christ. Everything else that vies to identify us must surrender to this.

In my work with pastors and churches, the challenge I have faced for many years is the discovery that – almost without exception – most pastors I meet for the first time find their identity in their role. They see their identity and value in being a pastor! It is no wonder that, if the pastors do not find their primary identity as a precious, beloved, redeemed child of our Abba, then the members of their congregation likely will not either. This is a big deal.

Identity gives clarity. One of the biggest obstacles to prayer for many followers of Jesus is misunderstanding who they are as children of their heavenly Father. Many who are fully redeemed by Christ's blood still see themselves as "sinners saved by grace." But this is not what our Abba says about us! Throughout the New Testament, the term "sinner" is never applied to those who are redeemed in Jesus.[8] In fact, the Bible refers to us as "saints" (which

---

8   The exceptions to this would be a mistaken identity, like the Pharisees lumping Jesus in with *tax collectors and sinners* (Matthew 11:19), calling Him a servant of Beelzebul (Matthew 12:22-28), or perhaps our recognition of Christ's work in us, like Paul calling himself the foremost sinner (1 Timothy 1:15).

means "holy ones")! The apostle Paul goes into great detail to describe our redeemed state in Jesus.

> *Blessed be the God and Father of our Lord Jesus Christ, who has blessed us in Christ with every spiritual blessing in the heavenly places, even as he chose us in him before the foundation of the world, that we should be holy and blameless before him. In love he predestined us for adoption to himself as sons through Jesus Christ, according to the purpose of his will, to the praise of his glorious grace, with which he has blessed us in the Beloved. In him we have redemption through his blood, the forgiveness of our trespasses, according to the riches of his grace, which he lavished upon us, in all wisdom and insight making known to us the mystery of his will, according to his purpose, which he set forth in Christ as a plan for the fullness of time, to unite all things in him, things in heaven and things on earth.*
>
> *In him we have obtained an inheritance, having been predestined according to the purpose of him who works all things according to the counsel of his will, so that we who were the first to hope in Christ might be to the praise of his glory. In him you also, when you heard the word of truth, the gospel of your salvation, and believed in him, were sealed with the promised Holy Spirit,*

*who is the guarantee of our inheritance
until we acquire possession of it, to the
praise of his glory.* (Ephesians 1:3-14)

Using Ephesians 1:3-14 as his reference, Tom Johnston shows people their new reality as redeemed children of God in Christ: "This is the truth about you! Blessed in Christ with every spiritual blessing, chosen, holy, blameless, predestined in love, adopted as sons and daughters, graced, redeemed, forgiven, and sealed with the Holy Spirit!"[9]

As "saints" in this life, we may indeed still sin, but sin is no longer part of our identity! When Jesus redeems us, that work is complete. Even as we yet struggle on this earth, our Abba sees us through the curtain of Jesus' blood, which blots out all our sin. All He sees is a precious child who bears the above description. We do not approach God in prayer as sinners, but as wholly and powerfully redeemed children whom He loves and upon whom He wants to lavish His blessings! Using kingdom "now, but not yet" language,[10] the apostle John writes:

*See what kind of love the Father has given
to us, that we should be called children
of God; and so we are. The reason why
the world does not know us is that it did
not know him. Beloved, we are God's*

---

[9] Johnston, *Alignment*, 14.
[10] See my discussion of George Eldon Ladd's kingdom explanation in the introduction of this book.

> *children now, and what we will be has not yet appeared; but we know that when he appears we shall be like him, because we shall see him as he is.* (1 John 3:1-2)

Johnston writes, "Identity is the core reality of who we are as created beings, bearing the image of our divine Father; and as his offspring, we are his children, his sons and daughters." He adds, "Only God can define us!"[11] Knowing who we really are changes how we pray; in fact, it changes everything. We approach God in love rather than in terror. We come as holy ones, not as sinners. We speak in intimacy, not in formality. We petition as beloved children. And in all this, we know we have our Abba's ear and heart!

> *I write these things to you who believe in the name of the Son of God, that you may know that you have eternal life. And this is the confidence that we have toward him, that if we ask anything according to his will he hears us. And if we know that he hears us in whatever we ask, we know that we have the requests that we have asked of him.* (1 John 5:13-15)

Knowing our heavenly Father as our Abba changes how we approach Him in prayer. Jesus invites us to pray to Him with real intimacy. We must remember that our Abba is our provider and protector. Our Abba gives

---

11 Johnston, *Alignment*, 13.

us our identity. We are precious, beloved, redeemed, provisioned, and protected members of His family. In these realities, we begin our prayer.

Putting It All Into Practice

Intimacy doesn't just happen; it is fostered through time and purposeful action. It is not natural for us in any relationship, and especially in our relationship with our Abba. Sin has made us resistant and rebellious. This must be intentionally overcome to build the prayer relationship described in this book.

Take time now and consider everything we have just laid out about God being our Father, our Abba. Be diligent to personally and truthfully answer the following questions:

1. How intimate is your relationship with God right now? Is your intimacy with your Abba what you want it to be? What steps could you take to grow in that intimacy?

2. How much do you genuinely love God? Do you love your Abba with all your heart? Do you love Him with all your soul (your will and emotions)? Do you love Him with all your mind (your thinking and intellect)? Do you love Him with all your strength? What steps could you take to grow in all of these?

3. How much do you truly trust God? Do you merely believe in your Abba with your head,

or have you trusted Him with your whole life? In what areas do you struggle to trust Him? What steps could you take to grow in the fullness of your trust toward Him?

4. How do you fear God? Is your fear negative (terror), or is your fear good and redemptive (reverence, awe, wonder)? How often are you "wowed" by Him in prayer? In what ways could you grow in your awe and wonder of your Abba?

5. In what ways do you depend upon God for your provision? Do you truly trust your Abba to be your provider?

6. In what ways do you depend upon God for your protection? Do you truly trust your Abba to pass His wings over you?

7. What is the current source of your identity (be honest with yourself)?

Jesus teaches His redeemed ones to pray to God as their Abba. Unlike today, when entire congregations recite the Lord's Prayer together (knowing full well that there may be people among them who have not yet surrendered to Jesus), the prayer was intentionally guarded for the first several hundred years of the church's existence. It was not introduced to people until they had confessed full faith in Christ and were subsequently baptized. This is because only the redeemed can call upon God intimately as their Abba. Thus, it was referred to as "the prayer of believers,"[12] and it still is.

Please do not rush on to the next chapter. Take the next seven days to grow in your intimacy with the Father. Make an action plan – put this into your daily schedule. Try to take an hour each day and devote it to time with your Abba. Don't give in to the need to talk. Be quiet. Learn to spend time just being with Him. Reflect on how He has provided for you during your lifetime. Reflect on how He has protected you. If there are frustrations in these areas, bring those to Him as your loving Abba, and listen with your heart for His response.

Then take some time to reflect on your answers to the questions above. Be real. Be honest. Bring all these to Him. If there is confusion or disappointment on any point, talk to Him about this. It may help to keep a journal. Writing out your prayers and questions is often a very impactful exercise. Be sure to leave space to record how God responds – how He moves and speaks and the scripture passages to which He takes you. Your goal here is not to give God your list of requests, but to grow in your intimacy with Him. Take your time. Be patient. Cut yourself some slack. Your Abba will meet you right where you are.

---

12   Jeremias, *Prayers*, 82-83.

Chapter 2

In the Heavens

Our Father in heaven, hallowed be your name. (Matthew 6:9)

Where shall I go from your Spirit? Or where shall I flee from your presence?
—King David (Psalm 139:7)

A First-Century View of Heaven

The Aramaic word for "heaven" is *shamayin* (similar to the Hebrew word *shamayim*). It can refer to the sky, the abode of God, or even the spiritual realm. Literally translated, it means "the heavens" (always plural). Keeping it simple, there are three typical parts to first-century Hebrew cosmology: the heavens (*shamayim*), the earth (*eretz*), and the realm of the dead (*Sheol*). Whereas our modern view of heaven is that it is a special place with God in eternity, Jesus' disciples would have held a broader definition.

To the first-century Jew, "the heavens" could mean

many different things, and sometimes they could mean them simultaneously. For example, the creation account shows us that *the heavens* included outer space, the realm of the sun, moon, and stars (Genesis 1:14). In addition, *the heavens* described the sky above us, where birds fly (Genesis 1:20). The same term is used by King Solomon as he prayed to dedicate God's temple:

> *Now therefore, O God of Israel, let your word be confirmed, which you have spoken to your servant David my father.*
>
> *But will God indeed dwell on the earth? Behold, heaven and the highest heaven cannot contain you; how much less this house that I have built! Yet have regard to the prayer of your servant and to his plea, O LORD my God, listening to the cry and to the prayer that your servant prays before you this day, that your eyes may be open night and day toward this house, the place of which you have said, "My name shall be there," that you may listen to the prayer that your servant offers toward this place.*
> (1 Kings 8:26-29)

Even when referring to God's dwelling place, it was understood that the heavens were inadequate to contain God. However, God had promised that He would descend to dwell in a temple made by human hands, and indeed

He did with the pillar of His shekinah glory resting over and filling its holy of holies (2 Chronicles 5:7-6:2).

For Jesus' disciples, "the heavens" surrounded them. Our God, our Abba, is uncontainable. When Jesus taught His disciples to pray "Our Abba in the heavens," it was an intentional recognition that our loving Father is everywhere. King David captured this glorious aspect of God's nature as he penned the lyrics to Psalm 139:

> *O LORD, you have searched me and known me!*
> *You know when I sit down and when I rise up;*
> *you discern my thoughts from afar.*
> *You search out my path and my lying down*
> *and are acquainted with all my ways.*
> *Even before a word is on my tongue,*
> *behold, O LORD, you know it altogether.*
> *You hem me in, behind and before,*
> *and lay your hand upon me.*
> *Such knowledge is too wonderful for me;*
> *it is high; I cannot attain it.*
> *Where shall I go from your Spirit?*
> *Or where shall I flee from your presence?*
> *If I ascend to heaven, you are there!*
> *If I make my bed in Sheol, you are there!*
> *If I take the wings of the morning*
> *and dwell in the uttermost parts of the sea,*
> *even there your hand shall lead me,*
> *and your right hand shall hold me.*
> *If I say, "Surely the darkness shall cover me,*
> *and the light about me be night,"*
> *even the darkness is not dark to you;*

the night is bright as the day,
for darkness is as light with you.
For you formed my inward parts;
you knitted me together in my mother's womb.
I praise you, for I am fearfully and wonderfully made.
Wonderful are your works;
my soul knows it very well.
My frame was not hidden from you,
when I was being made in secret,
intricately woven in the depths of the earth.
Your eyes saw my unformed substance;
in your book were written, every one of them,
the days that were formed for me,
when as yet there was none of them.
How precious to me are your thoughts, O God!
How vast is the sum of them!
If I would count them, they are more than the sand.
I awake, and I am still with you.
Oh that you would slay the wicked, O God!
O men of blood, depart from me!
They speak against you with malicious intent;
your enemies take your name in vain.
Do I not hate those who hate you, O Lord?
And do I not loathe those who rise up against you?
I hate them with complete hatred;
I count them my enemies.
Search me, O God, and know my heart!
Try me and know my thoughts!
And see if there be any grievous way in me,
and lead me in the way everlasting!
   (Psalm 139:1-24)

From the highest high to the lowest low, from the biggest big to the smallest small, God is there. "The heavens" describes at least three attributes of God that are absolutely critical to understand when we pray: He is omnipresent, transcendent, and immanent. God is everywhere at the same time, God is outside of His creation, but God is also right there with us at all times and in all seasons of life.

Our Abba Is Omnipresent

When we say that God is omnipresent, we mean that He is everywhere present at the same time. God's omnipresence is a companion attribute to His omnipotence (God is all-powerful) and His omniscience (God is all-knowing). Understanding that God is always everywhere has an enormous bearing on our prayers. There is no place one can go where God is not. No circumstance is outside of God's presence, remaining unknown to God. God has no spatial limitation – nothing is too big for Him, and nothing is too small. We've already looked at Psalm 139: God knows our thoughts, words, and concerns. He is present in both the heavens and in Sheol. He can lead and protect us in the depths of the sea. He is not blinded by any level of darkness. He is even with us in the womb.

Our Abba speaks through the prophet Jeremiah: *Am I a God at hand, declares the* LORD, *and not a God far away? Can a man hide himself in secret places so that I cannot see him? declares the* LORD. *Do I not fill heaven and earth? declares the* LORD (Jeremiah 23:23-24).

There is nowhere we can go, no situation we can face, where God is missing. We pray to a God who is always there. We pray to a God who is familiar with everything we face in life. All of creation belongs to Him, and He has influence over everything (Deuteronomy 4:39; Joshua 2:11). The writer of Hebrews reminds us: *Keep your life free from love of money, and be content with what you have, for he has said, "I will never leave you nor forsake you." So we can confidently say, "The Lord is my helper; I will not fear; what can man do to me?"* (Hebrews 13:5-6).

Our Abba Is Transcendent

When we say God is transcendent, we mean that He is greater than all creation. He creates everything that has been or will be created. He is not part of creation; rather, He made it and rules over it. Our loving Abba is separate from and independent of all creation. When praying to our transcendent God, I have been known to pray, "Only You are outside of this mess, so only You can fix this mess!"

Because God is separate from all He has created, He has understanding, plans, and interventions that we cannot even fathom. Speaking through the prophet Isaiah, God said, *For my thoughts are not your thoughts, neither are your ways my ways, declares the* LORD. *For as the heavens are higher than the earth, so are my ways higher than your ways and my thoughts than your thoughts* (Isaiah 55:8-9).

Because God is outside of all creation, He alone can understand everything with a view of the fullness of time. He can literally see both the beginning and the end of any situation.

> *Remember this and stand firm, recall it to mind, you transgressors, remember the former things of old; for I am God, and there is no other; I am God, and there is none like me, declaring the end from the beginning and from ancient times things not yet done, saying, "My counsel shall stand, and I will accomplish all my purpose," calling a bird of prey from the east, the man of my counsel from a far country. I have spoken, and I will bring it to pass; I have purposed, and I will do it.* (Isaiah 46:8-11)

As the Son of God, Jesus shares God's transcendence. Paul wrote to the Colossians, *He is the image of the invisible God, the firstborn of all creation. For by him all things were created, in heaven and on earth, visible and invisible, whether thrones or dominions or rulers or authorities—all things were created through him and for him. And he is before all things, and in him all things hold together* (Colossians 1:15-17).

There is literally nothing, even among the demonic forces, that is greater than our loving Abba.

Our Abba Is Immanent

When we say that God is immanent, we mean that our Abba is "within" all creation. This is not like the worldview called pantheism, which believes that everything is God and God is everything. God is not *part* of creation; He just chooses to enter *into* His creation for our sake. Think of creation more as a temple – separate from Him but designed for His purposes and glory.

God's immanence has enormous ramifications as to how we pray. God is with us. We can experience the fullness of His presence all the time – when we work, when we play, when we worship, and when we pray (Acts 17:28). All of life itself is in His hands (Job 12:10). His presence with us is complete: He is *over all and through all and in all* (Ephesians 4:6).

No matter how isolated we may feel, the reality is that we are not alone. In our praying, Abba is always with us. Remembering the beautiful intimacy we described in the last chapter, we have a prayer partner who has understanding and ability we cannot conceive. He exercises these with an unyielding love.

God exists both outside of time and space (transcendence) and within time and space (immanence). He can do this because He is everywhere present at the same time (omnipresence)! We are never alone.

Putting It All Into Practice

When one thinks of the kingdom timeline diagram we discussed in the introduction of this book, it is easier to understand the vast significance of our Abba's omnipresence, transcendence, and immanence in respect to prayer. Only a God with these qualities could span the space between the "now" and the "not yet." Only a

God with these qualities could dwell in the kingdom of God and still affect anything and everything about our existence in creation. Our Abba is both intimately present with us and infinitely unlimited in power and understanding. As the apostle Paul wrote to the Romans about the Holy Spirit's role in our praying, *If God is for us, who can be against us?* (Romans 8:31). Amen!

Take a few moments and think through the following questions:

1. Think about a time when you experienced the presence of God while you prayed. What happened? What steps might you take to increase the frequency of such experiences?

2. How does knowing that God is everywhere while you pray change your prayers for other people? For the needs of other cultures around the world? How much of your praying in the past has been to a God "out there somewhere" rather than an immanent friend?

3. When praying for someone who is resistant or otherwise "on the run," how does knowing God's omnipresent nature change the way you pray?

4. When faced with a monumental prayer need, how does your Abba's transcendence help you? Why is it important to know that God is separate from or above all of His creation as you pray?

5. In Psalm 139, the psalmist asks God to search his heart and to know him. How often do you invite God to scrutinize your heart like that?

6. Everything has been made by Jesus (John 1:3). Everything is sustained by Jesus (Colossians 1:17). How does this help us pray for correction and healing and in other circumstances?

7. Read 1 John 5:14-15. God is intimately present with us at all times and in all seasons. How does the fact that you know that He hears you impact your prayers?

Jesus teaches His disciples to pray with intimacy to the God who dwells outside of time and space, yet chooses to reside with us within time and space. He is not aloof. He is not uncaring. He has infinite understanding and ability. He is present everywhere, all the time. Our Abba is not the God of theological formulas and Torah gymnastics. He is right there with His children, all the time, and He loves them.

Make time in your daily routine to spend with your Abba. This is not a box to check, but is a relationship to develop. God is transcendent beyond all creation and is taking time to be with you. You must make time to be with Him. Review any expectations you have had for your prayer time. Investigate more of what the Bible says about God's omnipresence, transcendence, and immanence. Read the Bible passages that you discover regularly, or even commit them to memory. I suggest that you use a bound Bible instead of an electronic one;

Bibles on phones and tablets have too many distractions. Don't bring God your "prayer list." He doesn't work for you; it's the other way around. Have a conversation. This means that you will spend as much time listening as talking. Did you begin a journal for your prayer time as you read the last chapter? Keep it going, reviewing your responses to the questions above. These will likely plant seeds for many things you'll want to bring to your Abba in prayer.

Part Two

Kingdom Realities Today

Jesus declares a new society in the land. The long-awaited kingdom society will be marked by radical changes, and to express his vision for what God is about to do, Jesus clips lines from Isaiah's Servant song opening up Isaiah 61 and applies it to himself in Luke 4:18-19: The Spirit of the Lord is on me, because he has anointed me to proclaim good news to the poor. He has sent me to proclaim freedom for the prisoners and recovery of sight for the blind, to set the oppressed free, to proclaim the year of the Lord's favor.
—Scott McKnight, in *The King Jesus Gospel: The Original Good News Revisited*

Scripture is clear: humanity faces the choice between two kingdoms: the kingdom of God (the kingdom of light) and the kingdom of Satan (the kingdom of darkness). Jesus' prayer framework recognizes this, and He now leads His followers to invoke the authority they have been given as God's precious, beloved, redeemed children to call the realities of the kingdom of God into the world in which we live today.

Chapter 3

Be Holy, Your Name!

Our Father in heaven, hallowed be your name. (Matthew 6:9)

All worship is an intelligent and loving response to the revelation of God, because it is the adoration of His name.
—John R. W. Stott, in *Between Two Worlds: The Challenge of Preaching Today*

What's In a Name?

When I was a kid playing "cops and robbers" in Metro Detroit, we would yell, "Stop in the name of the law!" when apprehending bad guys and ne'er-do-wells. We probably got that phrase from Saturday morning cartoons, but the words have a historic meaning. Concerning policing in the United States and Britain, the "name" of the law spoke of the law as an ultimate authority in making an arrest. It reflects an earlier time when similar actions were done "in the name of the king." Likewise, the name of God represents His ultimate authority; in fact, it represents everything He is. We invoke this idea every time we pray in Jesus' name.

For the Hebrew people, one's name was distinctly personal. A name was not just a designation, but it communicated who he or she was – their character, experience, and identity. Describing how God breathed the breath of life into Adam's nostrils at creation (Genesis 2:7), messianic Bible scholar Warren Marcus writes:

> It is the Father who breathed into Adam's nostrils; He was imparting a portion of His very person to Adam.... It was G-D the Father imparting the essence of who He was to His created son, Adam. In Hebraic thought your *shem* (name) is your breath, and *your breath is your character.* It is your personality. It is what truly makes up who you are.[13]

Names are important throughout the Scriptures. God changed Abram's name in Genesis 17:1-8. He went from *Abram*, meaning "exalted father," to *Abraham*, meaning "father of a multitude," in keeping with God's covenant promise to make Abraham's descendants as numerous as the stars in the night sky. God similarly changed Sarai's name from *Sarai,* meaning "my princess," to *Sarah*, meaning "princess" (Genesis 17:15-16).[14]

---

13 Warren M. Marcus, *The Priestly Prayer of the Blessing: The Ancient Secret of the Only Prayer in the Bible Written by God Himself* (Lake Mary, FL: Charisma House, 2018), 83.

14 Sarah's name change doesn't seem significant, but it is. Whereas *Sarai*

Jacob came out of the womb holding the heel of his older twin, Esau. *Jacob* means "holds the heel," but was synonymous with "schemer" or "supplanter." He did some sneaky things to get his brother's birthright and blessing; but after Jacob wrestled all night with God (Genesis 32:22-32), leaving him permanently limp but knowing that he had personally encountered the Most High, God changed his name to *Israel*, which means "wrestles with God." This new identity was not just for the man, but became the identity for an entire nation. There is a notable New Testament example as well. In Matthew 16:13-20, Jesus changed the name of *Simon*, meaning "listening," to *Cephas* or *Peter*, meaning "rock." Peter would later grow into a whole new identity. The name represents the whole person.

The Name of God

The name of God is synonymous with His whole person. God's name is His self-revelation. God's name is His character. It is His self-representation and His authority.

God reveals Himself through His names throughout the Scriptures. We have already looked at Jesus' use of *Abba*, but see how vast our understanding of God's nature becomes as we review His other names:

- He is called *El Roi* in Genesis 16:14-15: "The One who sees me." God sees us in

---

shows that she is considered a princess within her own family, *Sarah* is universal – a princess over the whole world, if you will. This is likely how the tradition started that her name inferred she was "mother of nations," which turned out to be true. The new names given to both Abraham and Sarah gave them a universal status by God.

every situation, whether good, redemptive, challenging, or painful.

- He is called *YHWH Jireh*[15] in Genesis 22:14: "The LORD will provide" or "The LORD will see to it." As exemplified in His intervention as Abraham obediently attempted to sacrifice his beloved son, Isaac, God gives a deeply personal response in times of dire need. God meets us with provision in our time of desperation.

- He is called *YHWH Ra'ah* in Psalm 23:1: *The LORD is my shepherd.* This name is particularly precious as it speaks to God leading us to a place of authentic rest (sabbath). He provides nourishment, keeps us in shalom and on the right path, guides us in righteousness, and protects us from the dangers of life and predators.

- He is called *YHWH Rapha* in Exodus 15:26: "The LORD who heals you." This name speaks of healing and restoration.

- He is called *YHWH Nissi* in Exodus 17:15: *The LORD Is My Banner.* This name is

---

15   *YHWH* is *Yahweh,* the name God revealed to Moses at the burning bush (Exodus 3:1-14). It is given as "I AM WHO I AM" and is without any vowel pointing. Because the tense of a Hebrew word is found in its vowels, *YHWH* can also mean "I HAVE BEEN WHO I HAVE BEEN" and "I WILL BE WHO I WILL BE." The very name of God displays His eternality as the one *who was and is and is to come* (Revelation 4:8). Incidentally, when you see the word LORD in all capital letters in an English Bible translation, this specifically represents the name of God, *YHWH.*

multifaceted. It speaks of God being our standard (the flag under which we march), but also our covering, presence, protector, and victory.

- He is called *YHWH Shalom* in Judges 6:24: *The LORD Is Peace.* God is the God of everything meant by shalom: peace, tranquility, wholeness, completeness, perfection, prosperity, safety, and moving us to the good. It is God's ongoing work to take us back to what he declared "very good" in Eden before sin entered creation (Genesis 1:31).

- He is called *YHWH Tsidkenu* in Jeremiah 23:6 (also in Jeremiah 33:16): *The LORD is our righteousness.* God makes His people righteous. This relates to another name, *YHWH M'Keddesh*: *The LORD who sanctifies you* or makes you holy (Leviticus 20:8).[16]

- He is called *YHWH Shammah* in Ezekiel 48:35: *The LORD Is There.* God is present with us. Reflecting on what we reviewed in the last chapter about God's omnipresence, transcendence, and immanence, we see that His overwhelming presence is with us always and everywhere.

- He is called *YHWH Sabbaoth* in Isaiah 1:24 and Psalm 46:7: *The LORD of hosts* or "The

---

16 For clarification, the word *holy* means "set apart" or "reserved for God's special purposes." To be truly holy, God must also make us *righteous*, or "without guilt or sin."

Lord Almighty." This relates to another of God's names, *El Shaddai*:[17] *God Almighty* (Genesis 35:11). Our God is the God of heaven's armies. He is the God of all the inhabitants of earth (whether they recognize Him or not). This name expresses God's majesty, power, and authority. There is nothing He cannot do or accomplish.

- He is called *El Elyon* in Genesis 14:18-22: *God Most High*. This name expresses God's supreme authority and majesty. He has the absolute right to reign as preeminent over everything and everyone.

- He is called *El Olam* in Genesis 21:33: *The Everlasting God*. God exists entirely outside of time and space. He has no beginning and no end.

- He is called *Elohim*[18] in Genesis 1:1, referring to the one true God of Israel, and showing that He is strong and mighty. He is the God of creation.

Before we even get to the powerful wording in Jesus' lesson on prayer, we encounter God through the vast fullness of His name. He is Lord over all creation, eternal (unlimited by time or space), has the supreme right to

---

17 *El* is the Hebrew word for God. Whereas *YHWH* is His name, *El* is who He is.

18 *Elohim* is the plural form of the Hebrew word *El*. I believe this is an early reference to the triunity of our God, that He eternally exists in three persons: Father, Son, and Holy Spirit. *Elohim* is the three-in-one God.

reign, is almighty and commands the angelic armies of heaven, is ever present with us, makes us holy and righteous, bestows the fullness of shalom upon us, is our covering, protector, and victory, is our healer, provider, and loving shepherd, and sees us at all times and in all situations. God's name – God's self-revelation – shows us who He really is.

God's name also expresses His character. Beyond the names listed above, the Bible is replete with references to God's wonderful attributes: love, compassion, loving-kindness, grace, mercy, holiness, goodness (moral perfection), justice, wisdom, patience and longsuffering (patience under duress), omnipotence (all powerful), omniscience (all knowing), omnipresence (everywhere present), truthfulness, faithfulness, holy jealousy, immutability (unchanging character), eternality, immanence, transcendence, righteousness, incomprehensibility, self-existence, infiniteness, self-sufficiency (He needs nothing), personality, incorporeality (He needs no physical body), simplicity (He is not made up of parts), triunity (He is three in one: Father, Son, and Holy Spirit), sovereignty, and glory. All of these describe our awesome and majestic God. All of these, together, are realities that flow from the name of God.

The Grammar Is Important

As we now turn to three critical kingdom realities that Jesus teaches us to command – to literally call into existence – we have to first recognize an essential feature of the prayer's grammar: the use of third-person, singular, aorist imperative verbs for the first three stanzas. For most people, this sounds like boring gobbledygook. But it's not. It's not only fascinating grammar, but it actually changes the way we pray this prayer.

Jesus taught His prayer lesson in Aramaic, but it has been passed down to us in translations from Greek. The phrasing in Greek provides clarity on the level of prayer authority Jesus expects from those who pray this prayer. I am not going to write a Greek grammar here, but I do want to point out a few features that every believer should understand when it comes to this part of the disciples' prayer.

For example, this type of verb conjugation is not "normal" in English. We don't typically use third-person imperatives as they do in other languages. This means that English translations have to use a "work-around" in order for the phrases to make sense. Translators use helping words such as "let" and "may" to make the English translation work, but this actually softens some of the imperative nature. Concerning God's name, most English-speaking Christians pray this stanza of the prayer as "Hallowed be Your name" or "Let Your name be kept holy." But the actual Greek phrase here is "Be holy, Your name!" It is an imperative. Imperatives operate like a command. And it is in the third person. A second-person imperative would be commanding God to make His name holy. A first-person imperative would be commanding us (the ones praying) to make God's name holy. With the third person, it would seem that we are commanding God's name to make itself holy. However, there is a vital nuance we must not miss.

Third-person imperatives in Greek are used for unique emphasis. The Greek third-person imperatives can be used to command a "third person," but usually do not.[19] They are often a more stylistic way of expressing an imperative to the second person (in this case, God), softening the tone, or even to the first person (the one who prays).[20] We would not normally command God to do something; we work for Him, not the other way around! But the third-person imperative might be used in this way to fulfill the prayer mandate Jesus gives us in a holy and appropriate way – as if Jesus is teaching us that, in this instance, it is appropriate to make such a command of our loving Abba because it concerns the holiness of His own name. It is also possible that this grammar is used in an even softer approach, essentially commanding us to carry out what God desires – that His name is to be kept holy.

Nathaniel Erickson notes, "These petitions function like boomerangs: the directive force lands not on God, nor on the abstract notion of 'God's name/kingdom/will,' but on the prayers themselves! Jesus gives the command to those He is teaching to pray, and they re-give it to themselves over and over again."[21]

---

19 Nathaniel J. Erickson, *Translating the 3rd Person Imperatives in the Lord's Prayer, Part 2: the one praying is responsible,* October 17, 2024, https://ntgreeketal.com/2024/10/17/translating-the-3rd-person-imperatives-in-the-lords-prayer-part-2-the-one-praying-is-responsible/.

20 Glaze, Judy, "The Septuagintal Use of the Third Person Imperative," Master of Arts, Harding Graduate School of Religion, 1979.

21 Erickson, *Imperatives*.

The bottom line is this: Praying this prayer has the blessing of Jesus and wields authority to command certain kingdom realities into existence today. The grammar supports this, and it's a critical point as we take our next steps.

Praying the "Not Yet" into the "Now"

This brings us back to our kingdom timeline diagram. We discussed the two timelines in the introduction. There is the kingdom timeline (not yet on earth in its fullness) and there is the current timeline (here now, but corrupted by sin and under the influence of Satan's dominion of darkness).

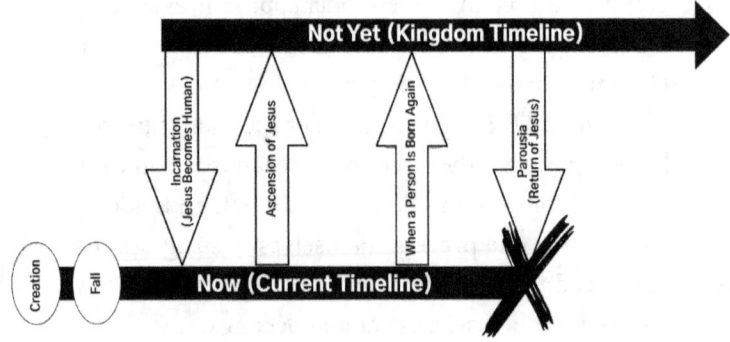

The Kingdom of God Is Now, But Not Yet

We'll speak about this in more detail in the next chapter, but understand that in His prayer lesson, Jesus is teaching His followers to pray that the realities of the kingdom timeline become true and powerful realities in the current timeline. We are literally given authority to call them from heaven to earth (hence, Jesus' statement, *On earth as it is in heaven*). And He begins with the holiness of God's name!

Be Holy, Your Name!

The word *holy* means "set apart." Human beings need to be made holy or set apart for God's purposes because we are born unholy (Psalm 51:5). Things in this world need to be made holy or set apart for God's purposes because they have been affected by humanity's sin. When a person surrenders to Jesus as Lord, Master, King, and Savior, that person is made holy. He or she is no longer identified with the utter sinfulness that condemns us all, but with the righteousness we are given by Christ (Romans 1:16-17). For each of us, our identity changes. We are no longer sinners, but saints (holy ones). We become our Abba's precious, beloved, redeemed sons and daughters. We still live on the current timeline, but from the point of salvation on, we are sojourners because we are full citizens of the kingdom timeline for the rest of eternity (Ephesians 2:19). And in that, we are "set apart" (1 Peter 2:9-12).

God, on the other hand, does not need to be "set apart," because He has never moved. He *is* apart. Holiness is about all of creation being restored to our Abba and His original intent. In the kingdom timeline – in heaven – everything is as it should be. But in the current timeline, it is not. The prayer, "Be holy, Your name!" is a prayer to make real in the *now* what is only true in heaven. And it is the very first petition Jesus instructs us to make.

God's name is His self-revelation. Our Abba wants all creation to know Him once again, but humanity generally does not recognize Him. When we pray, "Be Holy, Your name," we are not merely wishfully thinking. Robert Brandt and Zenas Bicket note:

> It is a genuine request, the first of a list of petitions: "Let Your Name [or Your Person] be treated as holy [or with reverence] among all mankind." This petition will be finally answered when God Himself sanctifies His name among all people in the coming Kingdom (See Ezekiel 36:22-23). Now our part is to balance our personal familiarity with a compassionate heavenly Father by showing complete reverence and respect. The Greek *hagiazo* means "to make holy," "to treat as holy," "to hold in reverence," "to highly honor." A person's name is more than a mere word; it stands for the person. God's name represents and signifies God Himself, including His character, nature, works, and words.[22]

If God's name (His person, nature, and character) remains unrecognized, then nothing else matters. The first three petitions in Jesus' kingdom prayer framework

---

22 Robert L. Brandt and Zenas J. Bicket, *The Spirit Helps Us Pray: A Biblical Theology of Prayer* (Springfield, MO: Legion Press, 1994), 218.

are about God, His kingdom, and His will. Ultimately, this prayer is about restoring humanity – and with us, all creation – back into a right relationship with God.

When we pray, "Be holy, Your name," we are praying for people everywhere to once again know our Abba. We are praying to grow in our relationship with Him as well. We are praying for humanity to come to know that they belong to Him. The psalmist sings:

> *Make a joyful noise to the LORD, all the earth!*
> *Serve the LORD with gladness!*
> *Come into his presence with singing!*
> *Know that the LORD, he is God!*
> *It is he who made us, and we are his;*
> *we are his people, and the sheep of his pasture.*
> (Psalm 100:1-3)

When we pray, "Be holy, Your name," we are commanding the realities of heaven to become realities on earth regarding God's nature and how humanity relates to God. Jesus is teaching us to have a truly eschatological view, looking passionately for the full revealing of God's coming kingdom in all of its holiness, power, and glory.[23]

> *Therefore say to the house of Israel, Thus*
> *says the Lord GOD: It is not for your sake,*
> *O house of Israel, that I am about to act,*
> *but for the sake of my holy name, which you*
> *have profaned among the nations to which*

---

23 Jeremias, *Prayers*, 98.

> *you came. And I will vindicate the holiness of my great name, which has been profaned among the nations, and which you have profaned among them. And the nations will know that I am the LORD, declares the Lord GOD, when through you I vindicate my holiness before their eyes.* (Ezekiel 36:22-23)

We are praying that God would once again be honored and recognized as the Almighty, the Eternal One, the Most High, and the Creator. We are praying that humanity – globally – would surrender to our Abba and experience the blessings of His peace, protection, provision, healing, deliverance, redemption, guidance, and victory. We are praying that every man, woman, and child would find their identity in Christ as precious, beloved, redeemed children of our Abba.

All of these things are true throughout heaven. All of these things are true for those of us who have surrendered to Jesus, who are now citizens of heaven (Philippians 3:20), and are residents on the kingdom timeline, even though we are living in the current timeline (John 17:13-18). Jesus teaches us to pray with kingdom authority and to command these realities into our own time. Jesus teaches us to pray with kingdom authority and to entreat our loving Abba to make them so. Jesus teaches us to partner with our Abba, walking in these realities ourselves, and introducing them to others through the gospel of Christ and the way we live our lives.

Putting It All Into Practice

To pray as Jesus taught us, we need three things: We must be in full surrender to Him as Savior and King, we must be growing in our relationship with God in all He has revealed Himself to be through the power of the Holy Spirit, and we must step out and exercise our God-given authority as His commissioned and authorized ambassadors on His redemptive mission. So this is where we must begin.

1. Honestly evaluate your relationship with your Abba. Is He just a wonderful theological concept you have accepted in your head as true, or do you have a real, personal, and growing relationship with Him as your Abba?

2. Honestly evaluate the state of your surrender to Jesus as your King. Does your whole life really belong to Him, or are you still reserving parts of it for yourself? What are you unwilling to yield to your Abba and His service?

3. Honestly evaluate your own holiness. Are you fully and willingly set apart for your Abba's purposes? Are you an active participant in His mission of redeeming the world? If not, what is holding you back?

4. As you review God's self-revelation as described in this chapter (His names and attributes), which of these have you come to know intimately? Which are still distant?

What steps will you take this week to deepen your relationship with your Abba in one of these traits?

5. Do you walk in the authority given you as Christ's ambassador? Are you consistently praying – *imperatively* – calling the realities of God's name to be fully established throughout humanity today? Are you praying like this for specific people?

6. Jesus' disciples would have prayed through this prayer at least three times every day. If such praying is to have the same daily significance for you as a follower of Christ, are you scheduling it? Are you protecting that time? If not, how will you begin?

Continue the work you started in the previous chapters. Grow in your intimacy with your Abba. If you began journaling, you will probably find it helpful to also journal about God's name. This will be especially true if you are praying for specific loved ones and friends. Continue growing in your practice of being quiet before your Abba. Grow in your ability to listen for His still, small voice in your heart and mind. Intentionally seek out scripture passages that relate to prayer. Read them reflectively and often. Memorize them. Take your time and let the Holy Spirit lead you.

Chapter 4

Come, Your Kingdom!

Your kingdom come, your will be done, on earth as it is in heaven. (Matthew 6:10)

The only way the kingdom of God is going to be manifest in this world before Christ comes is if we manifest it by the way we live as citizens of heaven and subjects of the King.

—R. C. Sproul

The Kingdom of God

It changed my view forever. It was 1989, and I was in seminary reading an assignment for my systematic theology course. Two books were required, and each profoundly impacted my understanding of Jesus and the kingdom of God. John Bright's *The Kingdom of God* showed me that Jesus was not merely my Savior, but He was, in fact, the King. He authoritatively established a new ruling order. Bright writes, "This, then, is the good news which the New Testament with unanimous voice proclaimed: that Jesus is indeed the promised Messiah, fulfillment of all the hope of Israel, who has come to set up the Kingdom of God among men.[24]

I was a relatively new believer at the time, although I had been raised in the church. I knew much of the Old Testament storyline, and I knew that Jesus was the Messiah (if only from the Christmas story), but somehow I missed the key point that He had come to establish the forever kingdom of God. The gospel is *the gospel of the kingdom* (Matthew 24:14). Jesus saved us, but our salvation is secure because He reigns! Bright shows that Jesus is the central figure of human history, with all of the Old Testament storyline leading up to His arrival, and the rest of history looking to His return in power and glory, coronating His everlasting kingship (Revelation 11:15; 19:11-16).

The second book was George Eldon Ladd's *The Gospel of the Kingdom: Scriptural Studies in the Kingdom of God*. It was Ladd who showed me that the biblical idea of God's kingdom was much more about God's rule and reign than a realm. That changed the way I read the Bible. When one realizes that most references to God's kingdom in the New Testament refer to God's dominion – His *kingship* – then kingdom verses take on a different meaning. Frankly, they become more powerful.

The whole Bible is about the kingdom of God, and Jesus is the main character of that narrative. He came to establish the rule and reign of God (Matthew 3:2; 4:17;

---

[24] John Bright, *The Kingdom of God* (Nashville: Abingdon Press, 1953), 190.

Mark 1:15). He proclaimed and taught the rule and reign of God (Matthew 6:33; 13:31, 44; Luke 13:18-21; 17:21; John 3:3). He demonstrated the power and authority of God's rule and reign as He systematically set people free from Satan's dominion of darkness – healing the sick; delivering the demonized; cleansing the leper; making the blind to see, the deaf to hear, and the dumb to speak; and raising the dead (Matthew 8:16; 12:15; 14:14; 15:30; 21:14; Luke 5:17; 7:11-17; Mark 3:10; 5:41; 6:56; John 11:1-57).

Ladd also helped me understand that while the kingdom rule and reign of God was ushered in when Jesus became human, the kingdom will not come in fullness until Jesus returns. This is the "now, but not yet" idea to which we have been referring in the earlier chapters of this book.

God created humanity in His own image and likeness (Genesis 1:26-27). Wayne Grudem translates this passage as, "Let us make man to be *like* us and to *represent* us."[25] God had always intended to share His rule and reign with humanity. He instructed Adam to fill, subdue, and rule over the earth and its inhabitants (Genesis 1:28). Of course, the fall of humanity in Genesis 3 was the ultimate rejection of God's rule, as well as our part in carrying it out on earth. From that point on, the Old Testament is the story of God working to restore His kingdom rule and reign, and humanity repeatedly rejecting God's kingship.

---

25 Wayne Grudem, *Systematic Theology* (Grand Rapids: Zondervan Publishing House, 1994), 442-443.

- The Tower of Babel was a rejection of God's supremacy (Genesis 11:1-9).

- The story of the Exodus has God's people complaining about God and rejecting Moses, God's leader (Exodus 2:14; Numbers 14).

- The Hebrew people had to wander in the desert for an entire generation because they rejected God's promised land (Numbers 13-14).

- The cycle of the Israelites in the book of Judges is a cycle of God's people repeatedly rejecting His theocratic rule (Judges 2:16-19).

- The Israelites' outcry for a human king (Saul) is a rejection of God as their king (1 Samuel 8, especially verse 7).

- Finally, God's ongoing instruction and correction through the prophets were also often rejected by His people. They even killed many of the messengers!

It is not until God Himself comes – Jesus – that the kingdom of God is finally reestablished.

John Bright writes:

> The New Testament announces with one voice and with unshakable assurance that all the hope of Israel has become present fact in Jesus Christ. It makes this assertion because it believed that in him the promised Messiah had come.... But if Jesus be

indeed the Messiah, that confronts us with a further question: what is the nature of his Kingdom? It is a question that follows inevitably. To acclaim anyone as Messiah is to announce in him the coming of the Kingdom of God, for it is precisely the business of the Messiah to establish the Kingdom.[26]

This brings us back to our kingdom timeline diagram.

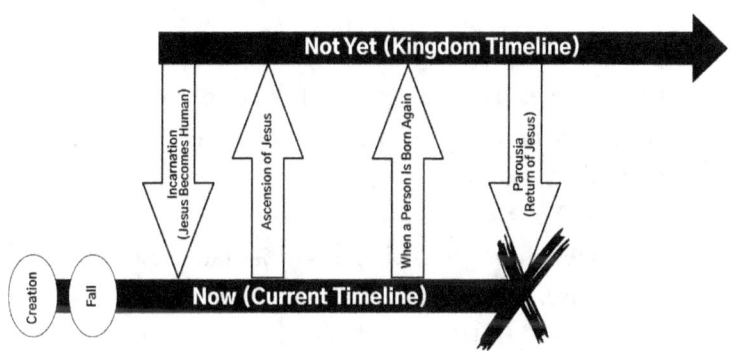

Jesus' incarnation (becoming human) was an invasion of sorts, with the kingdom of God laying siege to Satan's kingdom of darkness in order to rescue humanity. Since the fall, every man, woman, and child has been conceived in sin and born into sin's bondage (Psalm 51:1-12). Jesus' sinless life, sacrificial death, and glorious resurrection made it possible for people to finally be set free

---

26   Bright, *Kingdom*, 215.

from the kingdom of darkness and become citizens of the kingdom of light (Acts 26:15-18). They are in the world (in the "now") but not of the world (they are of the "not yet").

Jesus taught His disciples, and through them, all of us who currently live between His first coming (incarnation) and second coming (parousia), how to be citizens of God's kingdom and to pray that the realities of that kingdom would be established even *now* in our world. The first of those realities is God's name being holy now (see chapter 3). The second reality is just as profound.

Come, Your Kingdom!

Jesus teaches us to call for the full establishment of God's rule and reign *now*. Most English translations of the disciples' prayer say, "Let Your kingdom come" or "May Your kingdom come." But as we've already delineated in previous chapters, this statement is an imperative. Jesus tells us to pray, "Come, Your kingdom, Abba!" If we are God's children by redemptive adoption (John 1:12-13), and if as His children we have been commissioned with His authority to be His ambassadors (Matthew 28:18-20; 2 Corinthians 5:20), and if our loving Abba is truly omnipresent, transcendent, and immanent (see chapter 2), than He can do this and we have permission to command it!

We are citizens of the "not yet" kingdom of God living in the "now" – precious, beloved, redeemed children of the Most High God, calling for God's rule and reign to fully overtake **our lives**. The first territory to be offered is ourselves (Romans 12:1-2). When we pray, "Come, Your kingdom!" it is first and foremost a declaration that we surrender once again to our King. To pray, "Come, Your kingdom!" is to declare, "As your precious daughter or son, I am Your subject. I am at Your disposal." We pray for God's rule and reign over our hearts, our minds, our wills, our families, our homes, our personal resources, and more. Everything under our dominion must be surrendered to our Abba.

We are citizens of the "not yet" kingdom of God living in the "now" – precious, beloved, redeemed children of the Most High God, calling for the rule and reign of God to fully overtake **our churches**. As I noted before, nothing is more important than our King and His kingship. The church exists for the King's mission. To pray, "Come, Your kingdom!" is to declare that we, as God's congregation, submit all other agendas to the Immanuel agenda – to love God with everything we are, to love others as we love ourselves, and to make more and better disciples for Jesus (Matthew 22:37-40; 28:18-20). Our metrics are kingdom metrics. Our tactics are disciple-making tactics. We do not exist for ourselves, but for the people around us who are still stuck in Satan's dominion of darkness. In our surrender to the kingdom of God, every member of the body takes an active part in guiding people to become authentic citizens of heaven.

We are citizens of the "not yet" kingdom of God living in the "now" – precious, beloved, redeemed children of the Most High God, calling for the rule and reign of God to fully overtake **our cities**. If we are surrendered, and if our churches are surrendered, then this kingdom reality is a natural outcome. To pray, "Come, Your kingdom!" is to call God's rule and reign to overtake everything from our cul-de-sac to city hall. We are calling for God's dominion over our neighborhood, our village, our town, our city, our metropolitan area, and over all those who live in them. We are asking the Holy Spirit to bring our city leaders into surrender – first to Christ and then to God's kingdom will.

We are citizens of the "not yet" kingdom of God living in the "now" – precious, beloved, redeemed children of the Most High God, calling for the rule and reign of God to fully overtake **our countries**. To pray, "Come, Your kingdom!" is to declare God's kingship over the leaders of the land (1 Timothy 2:1-4). We ask the Holy Spirit to surround them with godly influencers. We ask the Spirit to convict them and guide them toward Christ. We pray that people throughout the land will humble themselves and surrender to God's kingdom (2 Chronicles 7:14-15). We pray for our Abba to raise up and send "missionaries" into all of the vital offices to guide our government according to God's will. We pray for revival for Jesus' church. We pray for awakening for everyone else.

We are citizens of the "not yet" kingdom of God living in the "now" – precious, beloved, redeemed children of the Most High God, calling for the rule and reign of God to fully overtake **our world**. To pray, "Come, Your kingdom!" is to pray like Habakkuk that *the earth will be filled with the knowledge of the glory of the Lord as the waters cover the sea* (Habakkuk 2:14). Just as in Habakkuk's day, we declare that the folly of our world will come to nothing, but that our King's redemption will be vast and unstoppable, to His glory!

Putting It All Into Practice

If we genuinely believe that nothing is more important than the King and His kingdom rule and reign, then we do not need to fear stepping into this prayer in faith. Take some time with the following questions and check your own heart.

1. How does your life reflect surrender to Jesus as "King of kings and Lord of lords"? How far does that royal title reach into your own life? If you feel discomfort with this question, ask yourself why.

2. How does your reading of kingdom passages in the New Testament change when you insert the word "reign" for "kingdom"? How does this understanding alter Jesus' many parables of the kingdom ("The kingdom of God is like . . .")?

3. What has been your primary understanding of the gospel up to now? Have you accepted a gospel of salvation, or have you truly understood that it has always been the gospel of the kingdom?

4. How have you understood Genesis 1:26-28? In what ways did God design us to rule over creation? Now read Ephesians 2:6. What do

you think *seated us with him* means? What about 1 Corinthians 6:3? What about 2 Timothy 2:12?

5. Describe your thinking about the two kingdoms (the kingdom of God/light and the kingdom of Satan/darkness; see Acts 26:12-18). What is your reaction to hearing God's expectation of you in the Great Commission to make disciples (Matthew 28:18-20)?

6. As we pray, "Come, Your kingdom," what is the Holy Spirit saying to you about your own level of surrender? Are there things about which you feel convicted? What steps do you need to take?

7. How will you pray, "Come, Your kingdom" for your church? In what ways is your church resisting the rule and reign of God? Is there resistance from any of the leaders? If so, how will you pray?

8. How will you pray, "Come, Your kingdom" for your village, town, or city? In what ways is your city surrendering? In what ways is it resisting? Do you know your civic leaders? How will you pray for them?

9. How will you pray, "Come, Your kingdom" for your country? In what ways do you see genuine surrender? In what areas do you see resistance? Do you know who your national

leaders are so you can pray for them by name? What will you pray for them?

10. How will you pray, "Come, Your kingdom" for our world?

11. Reserve some time this week to ask the Holy Spirit for guidance on praying in all these areas. If you began journaling, be sure to log your conversation with Him. Let Him lead you.

After teaching His lesson on prayer, Jesus continued by teaching about worry. Worry is a form of fear that usually exposes the reality that we do not fully trust God in some area. Jesus said that the solution is to *seek first the kingdom of God and his righteousness, and all these things will be added to you* (Matthew 6:33). Seeking God's kingdom is a reminder to surrender. Seeking God's righteousness is a reminder to act; righteousness is not just our "state" when we are in Christ, but it is also our lifestyle. If we are not seeking God's kingdom first, then nothing else matters.

As I noted before, Jesus' disciples prayed the disciples' prayer at least three times a day. This is a good practice for us as well. We all need regular reminders to remain surrendered to God. Why not set a reminder on your watch, phone, or computer and start praying this throughout the day? It will be a blessing to you.

Chapter 5

Be Done, Your Will!

Your kingdom come, your will be done, on earth as it is in heaven. (Matthew 6:10)

The will of God is not something you add to your life. It's a course you choose. You either line yourself up with the Son of God ... or you capitulate to the principle which governs the rest of the world.

—Elisabeth Elliot

God's Will and God's Kingdom

One of the biggest epiphanies of my life occurred when I prayed through the Lord's Prayer as a young pastor. As I experienced the conviction of the Holy Spirit and reckoned with the very personal ramifications of God's kingdom rule and reign over my life, the combined stanzas of the prayer – *Your kingdom come, your will be done* – stopped me in my tracks. I realized that if I believed in the present kingdom of

God – in His very real kingship over everything in my life – then I had to fully surrender to do His will. Period.

Jesus is our example. Once again, if we are to be Christlike, then we must emulate Him in yielding to the Father's will. John Wimber writes:

> In the Garden of Gethsemane, Jesus prays an echo of this prayer He taught His disciples, revealing a life trajectory set on honoring the Father no matter the price: *My Father, if it is possible, may this cup be taken from me. Yet not as I will, but as you will* (Matthew 26:39b). Jesus' will propels Him to ask the Father to take the cup of suffering and death from His hands. If He had stopped there in His request, who knows how the Father would have responded? However, Jesus adds the words "not as I will, but as you will," modeling for us our need to yield ourselves to the will of the Father – even as we honestly state to him the desires flowing from our own will.[27]

Surrender is indeed the key. If I surrender to God as my King, then I am, at the same time, surrendering to do my King's bidding. I must give myself fully to it. I must align with it and faithfully carry it out. I must recognize my Abba's inalienable right to rule. Paul wrote to the Christians at Rome:

---

[27] John Wimber, "Week 3: Your Will Be Done" in *The Lord's Prayer*, Vineyard Resources, https://vineyarddigital.org/item/the-lords-prayer/, 2014.

> *I appeal to you therefore, brothers, by the mercies of God, to present your bodies as a living sacrifice, holy and acceptable to God, which is your spiritual worship. Do not be conformed to this world, but be transformed by the renewal of your mind, that by testing you may discern what is the will of God, what is good and acceptable and perfect.* (Romans 12:1-2)

John Piper said that the aim of this passage is that "all of life would become spiritual worship."[28] That is true. Humanity is created for God's glory. To that end, Paul tells us that we can know the will of God, and that once we do, we are to present ourselves to carry it out. We must love the Lord our God with *all* of our heart, with *all* of our soul, and with *all* of our might (Deuteronomy 6:5; Luke 10:27). Glorifying God through our full worship is the ultimate expression of our love for Him. When one surrenders to the kingdom rule and reign of God, loving Him fully and glorifying Him through obedience and worship, then one can know and do God's good, acceptable, and perfect will.

Be Done, Your Will!

Your will be done. Too many times this phrase is uttered in resignation. When something painful or challenging happens, we offer this as a prayer of fate. But nothing could be further from Jesus' intent! As with the previous

---

28 John Piper, "What is the Will of God and How Do We Know It?" Desiring God, https://www.desiringgod.org/messages/what-is-the-will-of-god-and-how-do-we-know-it, August 22, 2004.

two kingdom realities, we are authoritatively calling the very will of God to be real and present in our "now." The presence of the kingdom rule and reign of God is not a state of resignation, but of glory. Paul wrote, *For the kingdom of God is not a matter of eating and drinking but of righteousness and peace and joy in the Holy Spirit* (Romans 14:17).

The presence of God's kingdom and His will together produce His very best intentions for us. There is righteousness; this refers to being in a right relationship with God and with one another. Yes, we are declared righteous by virtue of Jesus' blood, but we also *live* righteously with each other. There is joy; this refers not to happiness, which is circumstantial, but to the foundational gladness of heart that transcends one's circumstances. Happiness comes and goes, but the joy of the Lord remains steadfast, leading to unshakable hope.

There is also peace. Let's dwell on this. When it comes to the biblical concept of peace, something remarkable occurs. Both Hebrew (an Eastern language) and Greek (a Western language) share a nearly identical definition for peace. The fact that two such radically different cultures and languages would have a common concept of peace is in itself a miracle. It's like our Abba had a plan.

In Hebrew, the word is *shalom*. In Greek, the word is *eirene*. Both of these terms are translated as "peace" in English, but this is only one facet of an incredible definition gemstone. *Shalom/eirene* means many things simultaneously:

- Peace (lack of conflict)
- Tranquility (inner quiet, restfulness, calm)
- Completeness (We are settled in our identity as precious, beloved, redeemed daughters and sons of God in Jesus Christ.)
- Wholeness (deliverance)
- Finished (perfected)
- Health (healing)
- Safety (security)
- Well-being (authentic comfort, contentment)
- Prosperity (provision)

As I have tried to unpack these beautiful Hebrew and Greek words for my congregations over the years, I explain that they describe everything God called "very good" in Eden on the sixth day of creation. After completing His creative work on days one through five, God saw that it was "good" and gave His approval (Genesis 1:4, 10, 12, 18, 21, 25). But after creating humanity in His image and likeness on day six, God's appraisal was different.

And God blessed them. And God said to them, "Be fruitful and multiply and fill the earth and subdue it, and have dominion over the fish of the sea and over the birds of the heavens and over every living thing that moves on the earth." And God said, "Behold, I have given you every plant yielding seed that is on the face of all the earth, and every tree with seed in its fruit. You shall have them for food. And to every beast of the earth and to every bird of

> *the heavens and to everything that creeps on the earth, everything that has the breath of life, I have given every green plant for food." And it was so. And God saw everything that he had made, and behold, it was very good. And there was evening and there was morning, the sixth day.* (Genesis 1:28-31)

God looked over everything He had made in creation, including humanity, and He called it *very good*! God is saying, "This is excellent by My own standard. This is exactly what I had in mind. This is what I designed. This is precisely the way I wanted it. This is infused with My own nature. Humanity, the crown of My creation, is perfectly made in My image and likeness. This creation is the perfect environment in which humanity can flourish. This is *very* good!"

Shalom/eirene is the condition of what God called *very good* in Eden before Satan and sin corrupted everything. Think about it: no disunity or conflict, no illness or injury, no disorder, no oppression, no death; it is health, wholeness, well-being, tranquility, and pure relational connectedness with our Creator and each other. This is the ongoing experience of living in God's favor. This *peace* is the condition God intends to restore back to humanity in Jesus!

Paul said that the kingdom of God is characterized by righteousness, joy, and peace in the Holy Spirit. God's will is everything it takes to restore humanity to His kingdom. And while He will not force anyone to surrender against his or her own will, God doesn't want to lose any of us.

> *The Lord is not slow to fulfill his promise as some count slowness, but is patient toward you, not wishing that any should perish, but that all should reach repentance* (2 Peter 3:9).

> *First of all, then, I urge that supplications, prayers, intercessions, and thanksgivings be made for all people, for kings and all who are in high positions, that we may lead a peaceful and quiet life, godly and dignified in every way. This is good, and it is pleasing in the sight of God our Savior, who desires all people to be saved and to come to the knowledge of the truth* (1 Timothy 2:1-4).

Jesus teaches us to pray to our Abba, "Be done, Your will!" And just as with the kingdom, we must start with ourselves. When we pray, "Be done, Your will," we are asking God to align us fully with His will by the power and work of His Holy Spirit. We are echoing the prayer of our Savior: *Not my will, but yours, be done* (Luke 22:42). We are declaring our complete trust in Him – and such trust is a daily decision we each must make. (Similar to the father in Mark 9:24, I often find myself praying, "I choose to trust you, Abba. But please help me trust You more.")

English hymnwriter and theologian Frederick B. Faber reminds us, "There are no disappointments to those whose wills are buried in the will of God."[29] We are asking our Abba for His will to be done *in* our lives. In addition, we are asking our Abba for His will to be done *through* our lives. Ultimately, we are pleading with our Abba for His will to be done throughout all creation.

On Earth as It Is in Heaven

Be holy, Your name! Come, Your kingdom! Be done, Your will! The three kingdom realities we are entreated to call forth are all or nothing. God's name will not be truly holy (set apart among humanity) until His kingdom rule and reign are established. God's kingdom rule and reign only exist where His subjects faithfully carry out His will. Our Lord Jesus teaches us to powerfully pray for all three kingdom realities at the same time! This trifecta restores everything; it makes everything right.

Jesus teaches His followers down through the ages to pray with eschatological trust – with firm faith that their Abba will indeed bring full restoration and peace (*shalom/eirene*) as His kingdom is ultimately consummated. Joachim Jeremias writes:

> These petitions are a cry out of the depths of distress. Out of a world which is enslaved under the rule of evil and in which Christ and Antichrist are locked in conflict, Jesus' disciples, seemingly a prey of evil and death and Satan, lift their eyes

---

[29] Dwight L. Moody, *Thoughts for the Quiet Hour* (Chicago: Fleming H. Revell, 1900).

to the Father and cry out for the revelation of God's glory. But at the same time these petitions are an expression of absolute certainty. He who prays thus, takes seriously God's promise, in spite of all the demonic powers, and puts himself completely in God's hands, with imperturbable trust: "Thou wilt complete Thy glorious work, *Abba*, Father."[30]

We step out with our ambassadorial authority, and we pray for the establishment of God's holy name, for His kingdom rule and reign, and for His glorious will to be accomplished. Every time we witness injustice, we pray. Every time we see conflict, we pray. Every time we learn of injury, disease, or death, we pray. Every time we experience oppression, we pray. In our praying, we stand resolute as citizens of the kingdom timeline living as ambassadors in the "now." We are no longer *of* this world, but we are *in* it for God's purposes and glory.

The Kingdom of God Is Now, But Not Yet

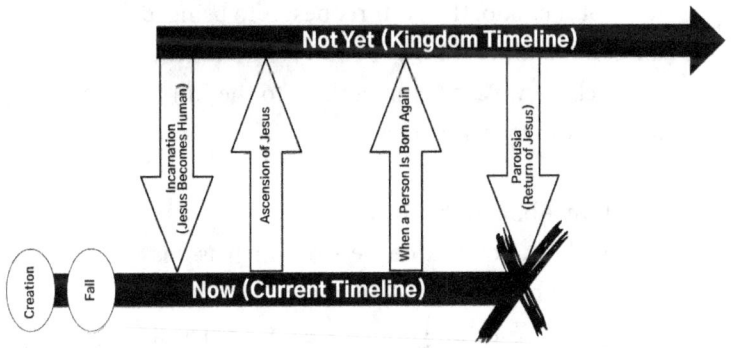

---

30   Jeremias, *Prayers*, 99.

When Jesus teaches us to pray, *On earth as it is in heaven*, He is giving us the priorities and authority to pray these three kingdom timeline realities into our "now." In heaven, our Abba's name is already set apart (holy). In heaven, our Abba already exercises full, complete, and unresisted kingship. In heaven, our Abba's will is always done. Think about it: When God speaks, how quickly do the holy angels who still surround His throne act? They respond immediately, thoroughly, faithfully, and without reservation. This is what we are asking for here on earth! In fact, in this prayer, we pledge ourselves to do the same!

In English, *on earth as it is in heaven* is typically seen as attached to "Be done, Your will." However, when one examines the Greek text, it becomes clear that grammatically, it is connected to *both* "Come, Your kingdom" and "Be done, Your will." I would take it a step further. I would argue that the call to make earth like heaven effectively applies to all three of the kingdom realities we are told to invoke. If, as I pointed out above, all three realities must indeed exist together or none of them do, then our request is to bring all three kingdom realities into our "now" simultaneously.

I believe we are being faithful to the full intent of our Savior when we pray:

> Our Abba in the heavens,
> Be holy, Your name, here on earth as it is in heaven!
> Come, Your kingdom, here on earth as it is in heaven!

Be done, Your will, here on earth as it is in heaven!

As we pray this way, we are partnering with Jesus to complete His mission to usher the kingdom of God into our world today.

Putting It All Into Practice

By now, your view of what we typically call "The Lord's Prayer" is changing. I hope you also see why Jesus began by telling us that we cannot pray this prayer for self-promotion (Matthew 6:5-6) or as empty recitation (Matthew 6:7-8). To pray for God's will to be accomplished in this prayer is to commit ourselves to be living demonstrations of faith-filled obedience.

Take some time and give yourself a prayerful pause. Let the Holy Spirit guide you as you respond to these questions:

1. If you now understand that the kingdom in this prayer is all about the rule and reign – the lordship, kingship, and dominion – of our loving Abba, what does this mean for you with respect to carrying out your Abba's will?

2. How surrendered are you, really? How aligned is your life and lifestyle to the kingdom and will of your Abba?

3. Describe how everything about our lives is to be "spiritual worship." How are you

consistently giving glory to God in your life? How are your love and faithful obedience right now?

4. How have you previously prayed, "Your will be done . . ." as an act of resignation or as a prayer of fate? How is the prayer that Jesus taught us supposed to be different?

5. What has been your understanding of "righteousness"? How has it changed as you read this chapter?

6. Describe your understanding of "peace." What has the Holy Spirit whispered to you as you learned the beautiful, multifaceted definition of *shalom* and *eirene*?

7. After reading this chapter, what would you say is God's will?

8. What do the words *on earth as it is in heaven* mean to you?

If the last three chapters have given you a lot of new truth to process, why not pause your reading for a while and just work on these? As we begin a new section, we're shifting from kingdom realities to our own critical needs as Jesus' disciples. The things we are taught to ask in the chapters ahead can only happen if the kingdom realities are true. Glory to our Abba: they are indeed true!

Part Three

Human Needs Covered

> God meets daily needs daily. Not weekly or
> annually. He will give you what you need
> when it is needed.
>
> —Max Lucado

As we call the realities of God's kingdom into our "now," we realize that we are redeemed kingdom laborers living in a still-unredeemed world. We need provision. We need the covering of our Abba's ongoing forgiveness. And we need protection in this battle – both from the devil and from ourselves.

Chapter 6

Give Us Tomorrow's Bread Today

Give us this day our daily bread,
(Matthew 6:11)

Many of the Lord's tracks overflow with abundance, but a special one is the track of prayer.

—Charles H. Spurgeon

Blessed to Be a Blessing

It's never been about us. But in the self-centeredness produced by the fall of humanity, we are now stuck in self-preservation mode. Before we revolted against our Creator, God's abundance was always readily available (Genesis 1:29). However, humanity's fall foisted rebellion on everything everywhere. What was once plentiful and available became unmanageable and scarce and required toil to harvest (Genesis 3:17-19).

Scarcity and hunger are the fruit of our surrender to the deceiver. Sin made life hard, but God had a plan.

As part of the kingdom realignment of humanity's heart, God established a spiritual principle. God would bless us, but that blessing was never for us to stockpile. A realigned heart is "other-oriented." God blesses us so that we can be a blessing to others. This principle was first declared to Abraham:

> *Now the LORD said to Abram, "Go from your country and your kindred and your father's house to the land that I will show you. And I will make of you a great nation, and I will bless you and make your name great, so that you will be a blessing. I will bless those who bless you, and him who dishonors you I will curse, and in you all the families of the earth shall be blessed."* (Genesis 12:1-3)

God blesses Abraham and his descendants so they can be a blessing. The fulfillment of this blessing and promise is ultimately found in Christ and His followers (Galatians 3:7-9, 27-29). God loves to lavish all kinds of blessings upon His children (Ephesians 1:3-14). The problem is that our self-centeredness has led to greed and corruption (James 4:3). The redeemed heart needs to learn to give again – to release and bless rather than hoard. It needs to learn to depend on God again for all our needs. This was the lesson of the manna after God's people crossed the Red Sea, free from four hundred years of slavery (Exodus 16:4-5). The Israelites were instructed to collect only enough manna for one day. Each day, they would get fresh provision. On the sixth day (the day of preparation for their Sabbath), they would collect two days' worth. But if they ever hoarded it, it became putrid and full of worms (Exodus 16:20).

The child of God needs to learn contentment, and that contentment is only produced in those who depend on God for everything. Paul knew this lesson well:

> *I rejoiced in the Lord greatly that now at length you have revived your concern for me. You were indeed concerned for me, but you had no opportunity. Not that I am speaking of being in need, for I have learned in whatever situation I am to be content. I know how to be brought low, and I know how to abound. In any and every circumstance, I have learned the secret of facing plenty and hunger, abundance and need. I can do all things through him who strengthens me.* (Philippians 4:10-13)

Contentment with dependence on our Abba is a powerful combination. Together, they address the biggest obstacles to our faithfulness: self-preservation, self-centeredness, greed, and the anxiety that drives them. Fear of lack is bondage. Contentment, trusting in God, is freedom. This brings us to the next stanza in Jesus' prayer lesson.

Prayer is typically focused on our own needs and the needs of those we love. There is nothing wrong with making such petitions to our loving Abba; however, that is usually the extent of most praying. Self-focused praying is yet another result of the self-centeredness discussed above. I believe that is why Jesus taught us to regularly meet with our omnipresent Abba and make His kingdom realities our first priority. Doing so causes us to pray for something bigger than ourselves. It is only after we invoke the utter holiness of God's name, plead for the establishment of His kingdom rule and reign, and call for His will to be accomplished above all else that we can begin asking for our own needs to be met. And in His kingdom prayer framework, Jesus emphasizes three needs in particular: our ongoing provision, our ongoing forgiveness, and our ongoing protection.

Give Us Tomorrow's Bread Today

Provision. God knows we need it, but we must embrace that need in the right spirit: contented and dependent on our heavenly Father, trusting Him to supply all our needs (Philippians 4:19).

Most English Bibles say, "Give us today our *daily* bread," but this is not necessarily the best translation. The problem is with the Greek adjective that we typically translate as "daily" – *epiousios*. This word is only used two times in all of the Bible – in the account of the Lord's Prayer in Matthew and Luke! R. T. France tells us that it is found in only one other piece of literature, a fragment of an Egyptian account book.[31] The term is

---

31   R. T. France, *Matthew* in *The Tyndale New Testament Commentaries*, ed. Leon Morris (Grand Rapids: Eerdmans, 1985), 135.

extremely rare, and there is no clear guidance on how to translate it. Grammatically, it might mean "daily," "future," or "tomorrow."

In his own research, Joachim Jeremias has found evidence from first-century Aramaic-speaking messianic Christians who used the Aramaic word *mahar* as they prayed this stanza; *mahar* means "tomorrow." They prayed, "Our bread for tomorrow, give us today." Jeremias also notes that church father Jerome, who was instrumental in translating the Bible into Latin, rendered the phrase as "bread for tomorrow."[32] Colin J. Hemer, research fellow at Tyndale House in Cambridge, England, also agrees with this conclusion.[33]

Jesus is teaching us to pray, "Give us tomorrow's bread today." There are two things we must say about this rendering. First, "bread" certainly refers to sustenance, but it is also commonly used for more general provision. Second, "tomorrow" certainly refers to "the next day," but also likely encompasses the kingdom future we have been describing. Let's look at each of these.

We have already noted that God loves to lavish every kind of blessing on His children. Those blessings can be physical (Isaiah 55:1), emotional (Philippians 4:7), spiritual (Ephesians 1:3-14), civic (1 Timothy 2:1-2), and national (Genesis 12:3). There is no reason to conclude that our Abba limits provision to food in this prayer. When Jesus teaches us to pray for "bread" each day,

---

32 Jeremias, *Prayers*, 100.
33 Colin J. Hemer, "ἐπιούσιος" in *Journal of the Study of the New Testament,* vol. 22, (1984), 81-94.

He encourages us to seek everything we need, both for life and for the fulfillment of His kingdom mission.

This was also Martin Luther's view. Speaking of Luther, John Stott stated, "Luther had the wisdom to see that 'bread' was a symbol for everything necessary for the preservation of this life, like food, a healthy body, good weather, house, home, wife, children, good government and peace, and we should probably add that by 'bread' Jesus meant the necessities rather than the luxuries of life."[34] I would agree. Again, we are to seek all that we need with contentment and dependence on our Abba. It is not that we should resolutely avoid luxuries, but they are not the subject of this prayer.

When we pray, "Give us tomorrow's bread today," we have the vastness of the kingdom timeline in view. Just as we have called for God's name to be holy, for God's rule and reign to be established, and for God's will to be accomplished here on earth as it is in heaven, so now we pray for the provision of the future kingdom to be real and available to us in the "now." John Wimber writes, "Jesus has requested the Father to bring to his people today some of the abundance of the Rule of God (from tomorrow). Give us today the bread we shall enjoy in the future in the Kingdom of God."[35]

Joachim Jeremias agrees:

---

[34] John R. W. Stott, *The Message of the Sermon on the Mount* in *The Bible Speaks Today*, New Testament Series, ed. John R. W. Stott (Downers Grove, IL: InterVarsity Press, 1978), 149.

[35] John Wimber, "Section 16: The Lord's Prayer" in *Teach Us To Pray*, vol. 5 (Stafford, TX: Vineyard Digital Resources, 1984), 89.

> In a world enslaved under Satan, in a world where God is remote, in a world of hunger and thirst, the disciples of Jesus dare utter this word "today" – even now, even here, already on this day, give us the bread of life. Jesus grants to them, as the children of God, the privilege of stretching forth their hands to grasp the glory of the consummation, to fetch it down, to "believe it down," to pray it down – right into their poor lives, even now, even here, today.[36]

Paul says, *God will supply every need of yours according to his riches in glory in Christ Jesus* (Philippians 4:19). That supply comes from our Abba's kingdom abundance! King David sings, *Delight yourself in the LORD, and he will give you the desires of your heart* (Psalm 37:4). Our Abba can give fresh, delicious water out of a rock in the desert (Exodus 17:6). Our Abba can prevent clothing and shoes from wearing out – even after walking for forty years in the wilderness (Deuteronomy 8:4). Our Abba can miraculously and consistently feed His prophet using a raven (1 Kings 17:6). Our Abba can make a widow's meager food supply last many days (1 Kings 17:13-16). Our Abba can turn water for ceremonial cleansing into the best wine anyone has ever tasted (John 2:1-11). Our Abba can take a boy's lunch and feed thousands of people, with more left over than when they started (Luke 9:10-17)![37] Our Abba can help

---

36 Jeremias, *Prayers*, 102.
37 The heading for this passage in all three synoptic gospels is "Jesus

His servant pay his taxes with a coin out of a fish's mouth (Matthew 17:27). Speaking of fish, our Abba can cause massive schools of fish to swim right into fishing nets – and He did it twice (Luke 5:1-11; John 21:1-14)!

The Kingdom Perspective

Jesus teaches us to ask our Abba for tomorrow's provision today. We seek the abundance of the kingdom to be provided in the here and now. But there is one more critical point to make: kingdom *provision* is given so that the kingdom *mission* continues. Abraham was blessed by God so that all the peoples of the earth could be blessed through him and his offspring. Our needs are met so that we can stay the course – making our Abba known, proclaiming our Abba's rule and reign, demonstrating our Abba's authority, and carrying out our Abba's will undaunted. Paul wrote to the Christians at Corinth:

> *He who supplies seed to the sower and bread for food will supply and multiply your seed for sowing and increase the harvest of your righteousness. You will be enriched in every way to be generous in every way, which through us will produce thanksgiving to God. For the ministry of this service is not only supplying the needs of the saints*

Feeds the Five Thousand," but the text makes clear that this was just the number of men. With women and children present, some estimate the crowd could easily have been three times that number! And they still had twelve baskets of broken pieces left over (Luke 9:17)!

> *but is also overflowing in many thanksgivings to God. By their approval of this service, they will glorify God because of your submission that comes from your confession of the gospel of Christ, and the generosity of your contribution for them and for all others, while they long for you and pray for you, because of the surpassing grace of God upon you. Thanks be to God for his inexpressible gift!* (2 Corinthians 9:10-15)

The Corinthians' gift, which is provision for Paul's fellow laborers, produces enormous fruit for their Abba's mission: a harvest of righteousness, praise and thanksgiving to God, glory to God (worship), and intercessory prayer! Yes, our needs are met, but this is not for ourselves; it is for the kingdom's advancement. We are blessed to be a blessing!

Human Needs Covered

After we have invoked the three kingdom realities given in Jesus' kingdom prayer framework, we are instructed to pray that three of our most critical needs will be met:

1. We pray for provision with an aligned heart that is not greedy or self-centered.

2. We pray for forgiveness with an aligned heart that continually forgives and exemplifies forgiveness to others.

3. We pray for protection with an aligned heart that keeps us focused on the task of unseating the devil and his works.

We will look at our needs for forgiveness and protection in the following two chapters. In the meantime, we pray that our hearts remain aligned with the heart of our loving Abba. We pray that we remain content, dependent, and wonderfully anxiety-free about our daily provision. We don't worry about the mortgage, the car payment, the grocery bill, the price of gas, the student loan, etc. because Jesus tells us, *Seek first the kingdom of God and his righteousness, and all these things will be added to you* (Matthew 6:33).

Putting It All Into Practice

We have said that this is a kingdom prayer prayed by kingdom people with kingdom authority for the kingdom mission. I hope you're beginning to see the importance of that perspective. The disciples' prayer is a powerful and authoritative weapon for kingdom advancement. It enables Jesus' disciples (ancient and modern) to participate vitally in redeeming humanity and all creation. However, this stanza also reveals the work of redemption within ourselves. There is no better barometer of the depth of our discipleship than our perspective on our provision.

Take some time and prayerfully consider the following questions:

GIVE US TOMORROW'S BREAD TODAY

1. Why are we humans so enamored with money? With our stuff?

2. On a scale from 1 to 10, with 1 being "Not at All" and 10 being "Yep, You Nailed Me," how deep is the bondage you feel to your provision? How much do you worry about paying the bills? The economy? Having enough?

3. We're blessed to be a blessing. How consistently do you bless others with your own provision (money, food, home, car, etc.)?

4. Describe your current level of contentment. Has it increased or decreased during the past few years? Why?

5. Describe your *actual* dependence on God for your provision. What does your level of trust look like?

6. When you pray, how much of your prayer "list" is focused on your own needs and the needs of those you love? How much of it is really about the kingdom?

7. What is your honest reaction to the knowledge that your Abba puts His kingdom abundance at your disposal? When you think about that, how tempted are you to want luxury? To hoard?

8. As you review the many biblical examples given of God's abundance, do you believe He still does such things? Why or why not?

9. How much does your Abba's kingdom mission's advancement depend on you? Why?

10. What steps do you need to take to make this stanza of the disciples' prayer a daily priority in your life? When will you start?

Are you journaling? It might be helpful to process your answers to these questions in writing. You might even want to work through them with a partner; it could help you both.

Chapter 7

Forgive Us As We Forgive Others

And forgive us our debts, as we also have forgiven our debtors. (Matthew 6:12)

To be a Christian means to forgive the inexcusable because God has forgiven the inexcusable in you.

—C. S. Lewis

The Heart of Our Faith

We now turn to the second critical need we face as our Abba's kingdom people. We need His forgiveness all the time, every single day. Forgiveness is the heart of the Christian faith. Everything about our redemption centers on our heavenly Father's loving act of forgiveness. Everything. Therefore, one cannot be a follower of Jesus and withhold forgiveness toward anyone. Period.

After James, the half brother of Jesus, became the lead apostle of the church in Jerusalem, he wrote his famous letter to Jewish Christians who were spread all over the Roman Empire. In this letter, he makes some scathing remarks toward his readers:

> *What causes quarrels and what causes fights among you? Is it not this, that your passions are at war within you? You desire and do not have, so you murder. You covet and cannot obtain, so you fight and quarrel. You do not have, because you do not ask. You ask and do not receive, because you ask wrongly, to spend it on your passions. You adulterous people! Do you not know that friendship with the world is enmity with God? Therefore whoever wishes to be a friend of the world makes himself an enemy of God. Or do you suppose it is to no purpose that the Scripture says, "He yearns jealously over the spirit that he has made to dwell in us"? But he gives more grace. Therefore it says, "God opposes the proud but gives grace to the humble." Submit yourselves therefore to God. Resist the devil, and he will flee from you. Draw near to God, and he will draw near to you. Cleanse your hands, you sinners, and purify your hearts, you double-minded. Be wretched and mourn and weep. Let your laughter be turned to mourning and your joy to gloom. Humble yourselves before the Lord, and he will exalt you.* (James 4:1-10)

You adulterous people! Wow! We need to understand the context of James' wrath. James chose his words with full intentionality. Adultery is a violation of a covenant. His readers are Jewish people who have accepted Jesus as the Messiah. Unlike the growing number of Gentile Christians, Jewish Christians are steeped in covenant life. They have always been a covenant people (Genesis 15:1-21). They have the Scriptures (at that time, what we would call the Old Testament), which attest to all that the Messiah would accomplish. They have the prophets, who were very specific about what God required, and some of whom even outlined the coming new covenant. Of all people on earth, James' readers should know better.

Jesus, the Christ (Messiah), is the second person of the triune Godhead. With the Father and the Holy Spirit, Jesus embodied all of the attributes of God (see chapter 3). Jesus dwelt in glory. Jesus sat in the throne room of the heavens. And because of pure self-sacrificing love, Jesus left all of that to redeem humanity (John 3:16-17). Jesus voluntarily took on all the limitations of human flesh, including the ability to be put to death (Philippians 2:6-8). He suffered betrayal (Luke 22:48), abandonment (Mark 14:50), denial (Luke 22:54-62), beating and insult (Luke 22:63-65), and horrific scourging (Matthew 27:26; Mark 15:15; John 19:1). He then was executed in the most heinous, painful way possible: crucifixion (John 19:16-30). And all of this was to take the sins of humanity upon Himself once and for all (Isaiah 53:1-12; 2 Corinthians 5:21; 1 Peter 2:22-25; Hebrews 10:10).

In paying the penalty for our sin, Jesus instituted a new covenant between God and those who surrender to Him (Jeremiah 31:31-34; Luke 22:20; Hebrews 8:1-13). This new covenant relationship is eternal. It is the eternal life God has promised in Christ (John 3:16-17; 10:28-30; 2 Corinthians 4:17; 1 John 5:11-13; Revelation 21:3-4). All of this requires full forgiveness and restoration between us and our loving Abba.

Jesus did not need to do any of this. He did it voluntarily (John 10:18). Jesus went through the agony and paid the penalty to establish forgiveness, reconciliation, and peace, which leads us back to James' readers. They were a covenant people. They were aware of the entire history that led up to Christ's sacrifice. They were familiar with the sacrificial system and its requirements for forgiveness. Of all people, they understood the cost of sin, the sacrifice to atone for it, the work of the Messiah, and the new-covenant relationship it established. And of all people, they were refusing to forgive one another! James calls them out, saying that it is nothing short of unfaithfulness to Christ! They were violating the new covenant.

Not Allowed to Not Forgive

James' letter shows us how seriously our Abba takes the matter of forgiveness. It is the very heart of the Christian faith. To withhold forgiveness toward anyone is to deny the faith and the incredible sacrifice our Savior made to establish it. In essence, it is a rejection of God (His name), the kingdom (His reign), and His plan for us (His will). We cannot *not* forgive. Paul wrote to the Ephesians, *Let all bitterness and wrath and anger and clamor and slander be put away from you, along with all malice. Be kind to one another, tenderhearted, forgiving one another, as God in Christ forgave you* (Ephesians 4:31-32).

Paul wrote to the Colossians, *Put on then, as God's chosen ones, holy and beloved, compassionate hearts, kindness, humility, meekness, and patience, bearing with one another and, if one has a complaint against another, forgiving each other; as the Lord has forgiven you, so you also must forgive* (Colossians 3:12-13).

We are not allowed to *not* forgive. We are to forgive each other just as God, in Christ, forgave us. Jesus drove this point home to Peter and the rest of His disciples as Peter asked how many times he had to forgive someone. In response, Jesus told them all the powerful parable of the unmerciful servant:

> *Then Peter came up and said to him, "Lord, how often will my brother sin against me, and I forgive him? As many as seven times?" Jesus said to him, "I do not say to you seven times, but seventy-seven times.*
>
> *"Therefore the kingdom of heaven may be compared to a king who wished to settle accounts with his servants. When he began to settle, one was brought to him who owed him ten thousand talents. And since he could not pay, his master ordered him to be sold,*

with his wife and children and all that he had, and payment to be made. So the servant fell on his knees, imploring him, 'Have patience with me, and I will pay you everything.' And out of pity for him, the master of that servant released him and forgave him the debt. But when that same servant went out, he found one of his fellow servants who owed him a hundred denarii, and seizing him, he began to choke him, saying, 'Pay what you owe.' So his fellow servant fell down and pleaded with him, 'Have patience with me, and I will pay you.' He refused and went and put him in prison until he should pay the debt. When his fellow servants saw what had taken place, they were greatly distressed, and they went and reported to their master all that had taken place. Then his master summoned him and said to him, 'You wicked servant! I forgave you all that debt because you pleaded with me. And should not you have had mercy on your fellow servant, as I had mercy on you?' And in anger his master delivered him to the jailers, until he should pay all his debt. So also my heavenly Father will do to every one of you, if you do not forgive your brother from your heart" (Matthew 18:21-35).

The master in the story turns the wicked servant over to the jailers (the word in Greek is actually "torturers") until he paid all that he owed. In other words, because the size of the debt was literally unpayable, he would be tortured forever. This is a picture of hell. Jesus ended the teaching with these words: *So also my heavenly Father will do to every one of you, if you do not forgive your brother from your heart* (Matthew 18:35). We do not withhold forgiveness. Our Abba is not fooling around on this point.

Forgive Us as We Forgive Others

In his prayer framework, Jesus teaches us to pray, *Forgive us our debts, as we also have forgiven our debtors.* There is a foolish debate that sometimes arises between those who say "debts" (as in Matthew's gospel) and those who say "trespasses" or "sins" (as in Luke's gospel). It is important to note, however, that Luke then goes on to say, *For we ourselves forgive everyone who is indebted to us* (Luke 11:4). Some English translations say, "who sins against us," or "who trespasses against us." But the Greek clearly uses the word for debt. Joachim Jeremias explains that the matter is clarified when one examines the Aramaic word Jesus would have used: *hobha.* This word literally means "something owed."[38] Sin exacts a price. There is a cost. Jesus redeemed us (Romans 3:24; Ephesians 1:7; Galatians 3:13). We have been purchased by His blood (1 Corinthians 6:20; 1 Peter 1:18-19). Forgiveness is releasing a debt.

Further, Jeremias adds that the present perfect form of *as we also have forgiven our debtors* is a poor translation,

---

38   Jeremias, *Prayers*, 92.

because *present* perfect is *present* action. It is better translated as "as we are *even now* forgiving our debtors."[39]

Jesus teaches us to ask our Abba to forgive us *as* we are forgiving those who have sinned against us. We ask our Abba to forgive us *in the same way as* we are forgiving those who are indebted to us. Think about that person in your life who has hurt you, frustrated you, or violated you the most. Jesus teaches us to ask our loving Abba to forgive us *exactly as we are forgiving that person!* To further drive the point home, in the Sermon on the Mount version of His prayer lesson, Jesus ended the prayer with this stark reminder: *For if you forgive others their trespasses, your heavenly Father will also forgive you, but if you do not forgive others their trespasses, neither will your Father forgive your trespasses* (Matthew 6:14-15).

Again, He doesn't take the matter of forgiveness lightly.

Defining Forgiveness

I have found that many Christians understand that they must forgive others, but they are unclear about what that forgiveness entails. This is an indictment of the church for not teaching people the practicalities of forgiveness. One of the best definitions I have seen on forgiveness comes from the seminal work of Ken Sande on biblical peacemaking. In his book *The Peacemaker*, Ken provides four promises of forgiveness. When we say, "I forgive you," we are making these promises:

---

39 Jeremias, *Prayers*, 92.

1. I promise I will not dwell on this incident.
2. I promise I will not bring up this incident and use it against you.
3. I promise I will not talk to others about this incident.
4. I promise I will not allow this incident to stand between us or hinder our personal relationship.[40]

These promises are modeled after God's forgiveness of us. While the fourth promise assumes that an ongoing personal relationship is possible and safe, although it genuinely may not be, these are otherwise the very promises our Abba makes to each of us when we turn to Christ for forgiveness and salvation. He extends grace and mercy to us; we must extend the same grace and mercy to those who hurt us, and this without exception.

Putting It All Into Practice

Forgiveness is nonnegotiable. We must ask for it when needed, and we must give it when offended. Jesus gave this stanza in His prayer framework because we cannot be kingdom citizens without it.

As you read this chapter, what is the Holy Spirit saying to you? Prayerfully consider these questions as you process your own walk of forgiveness with your Abba:

---

[40] Ken Sande, *The Peacemaker: A Biblical Guide to Resolving Personal Conflict* (Grand Rapids: Baker Books, 2004), 209.

1. How am I forgiving others? (This should be a daily inventory!)

2. Who do I need to forgive today? If I am resisting, why?

3. What are the wounds that keep coming back up in my mind? Spend time with God to discern if you still need to grant forgiveness or if this is a matter of healing that is yet to come.

4. What things do I simply need to release to my heavenly Father and not take back from Him?

5. Who do I need to ask to forgive me? Who have I sinned against? If I am resisting, why?

6. What have I done for which I need to ask my Abba's forgiveness?

7. How have I resisted God? What aspects of His name am I avoiding?

8. How have I resisted His kingdom? What areas of my life are still not surrendered to His loving rule and reign?

9. How have I resisted His will?

10. How have I sinned against my Abba in thought, word, or deed? (Review 1 John 1:9.)

11. Consider the warning of Matthew 6:14-15. How am I sabotaging my ability to walk daily in God's forgiveness by withholding it from others?

12. What other things has the Holy Spirit revealed to me in this chapter that I must address?

Spend some time quietly with your Abba on this topic. Use your journal or a notepad to begin writing down all the people in your life who have hurt you, betrayed you, undermined you, or otherwise abused you. Now pray through those names one by one and release them in forgiveness. If you struggle to do this with some of them, talk to a confidant who understands biblical forgiveness, and ask for help. It may take time, but ultimately, you are not allowed to withhold forgiveness from anyone.

Chapter 8

Protect Us from Evil

And lead us not into temptation, but deliver us from evil. (Matthew 6:13)

> Have we trials and temptations?
>   Is there trouble anywhere?
> We should never be discouraged—
>   Take it to the Lord in prayer.
> —Joseph M. Scriven,
> *What a Friend We Have in Jesus*

Our Three Great Needs

Jesus' prayer lesson for His followers began with a clear recognition of who God is. It then leads the one praying to invoke three kingdom realities into our "now": the holiness of God's name, the establishment of God's kingdom, and the faithful execution of God's will. Jesus ended His prayer lesson by showing us how to pray for our own three great ongoing needs: provision, forgiveness, and protection – all of which are blessings of the coming kingdom. John Stott rightly said:

> Thus the three petitions which Jesus puts upon our lips are beautifully comprehensive. They cover, in principle, all our human need – material (daily bread), spiritual (forgiveness of sins) and moral (deliverance from evil). What we are doing whenever we pray this prayer is to express our dependence upon God in every area of our human life. Moreover, a trinitarian Christian is bound to see in these three petitions a veiled allusion to the Trinity, since it is through the Father's creation and providence that we receive our daily bread, through the Son's atoning death that we may be forgiven, and through the Spirit's indwelling power that we are rescued from the evil one.[41]

We have looked at the first two great needs; now we conclude with the third one, which has two distinct but inextricably related parts: our own temptations and the plans of the Evil One.

The Battle Is Real

We've already stated that there are two opposing kingdoms: the kingdom of God (kingdom of light) and the

---

41 Stott, *Message*, 150-151.

kingdom of Satan (kingdom of darkness). The moment we are conceived, every human being is already in the battle. We are at war, and we are subjects of one kingdom or the other; there is no neutral territory. But the battle did not start with us. The rebellion actually started in heaven. Can you believe it? The prophets Isaiah and Ezekiel give us some insight.

Satan (whose very name means "adversary" in Hebrew)[42] was not created evil. God calls him *Heylel*, which means "morning star" or "day star" in his original, sin-free condition. In Latin, this name is *Lucifer* or "light bearer." So when you hear people refer to him as Lucifer, this is only appropriate in his pre-evil state. God arguably created *Heylel* as the most beautiful being of all creation! Look at this description:[43]

> *Moreover, the word of the LORD came to me:*
> *"Son of man, raise a lamentation over the king of Tyre, and say to him, Thus says the Lord GOD:*
> *'You were the signet of perfection,*
> *full of wisdom and perfect in beauty.*
> *You were in Eden, the garden of God;*
> *every precious stone was your covering,*
> *sardius, topaz, and diamond,*
> *beryl, onyx, and jasper,*
> *sapphire, emerald, and carbuncle;*

---

42 The monicker "devil" actually comes from the Greek term for him, "Diabolos."

43 God gives the prophet Ezekiel a lament over the King of Tyre. This king is so incredibly evil that he has become a "type" of Satan himself. And as the prophet proclaims God's lament, we get a glimpse into Satan's fall.

and crafted in gold were your settings
and your engravings.
On the day that you were created
they were prepared.
You were an anointed guardian cherub.
I placed you; you were on the holy mountain
    of God;
in the midst of the stones of fire you walked.
You were blameless in your ways
from the day you were created,
till unrighteousness was found in you.
In the abundance of your trade
you were filled with violence in your midst,
    and you sinned;
so I cast you as a profane thing from the
    mountain of God,
and I destroyed you, O guardian cherub,
from the midst of the stones of fire.
Your heart was proud because of your
    beauty;
you corrupted your wisdom for the sake of
    your splendor.
I cast you to the ground;
I exposed you before kings,
to feast their eyes on you.
By the multitude of your iniquities,
in the unrighteousness of your trade
you profaned your sanctuaries;
so I brought fire out from your midst;
it consumed you,
and I turned you to ashes on the earth

in the sight of all who saw you.
All who know you among the peoples
are appalled at you;
you have come to a dreadful end
and shall be no more forever."
(Ezekiel 28:11-19)

Perfection. Full of wisdom. Perfect in beauty. Adorned with every precious stone. Settings crafted of gold. Anointed guardian cherub.[44] This description leads many theologians to believe that he may have been designed to lead worship in heaven, as his very being appears created to beautifully reflect and refract the glory of God. In fact, this may have been the source of his prideful downfall. Ezekiel tells us that his heart became proud because of his beauty, and his wisdom was corrupted because of his splendor. What he apparently neglected to understand, however, was that this beauty and splendor did not come from him. Just as a diamond only sparkles in the light, so he was only splendid when basking in the glory of God.

As Isaiah prophesied about the king of Babylon, he gives us more insight into *Heylel's* rebellion:[45]

How you are fallen from heaven,
O Day Star, son of Dawn!
How you are cut down to the ground,
you who laid the nations low!

---

[44] Satan is of the cherubim, which are ranking angelic beings involved in the worship and service of God.

[45] Another earthly king so evil that he becomes a prophetic "type" of Satan.

> *You said in your heart,*
> *"I will ascend to heaven;*
> *above the stars of God*
> *I will set my throne on high;*
> *I will sit on the mount of assembly*
> *in the far reaches of the north;*
> *I will ascend above the heights of the clouds;*
> *I will make myself like the Most High."*
> *But you are brought down to Sheol,*
> *to the far reaches of the pit.*
> (Isaiah 14:12-15)

Those five "I will" statements are Satan's progression of evil. The created one set his sights on overthrowing the Creator! He wanted God's *position*. He wanted God's *authority*. He wanted God's *throne*. He wanted God's *worship*. He wanted to *become* God. But God said, "Nope!" And the Almighty cast him out of heaven, changing his name and consigning him to the place of the dead.

This bit of "heavenly history" is vital because it sets the stage for the battle we find ourselves in. When God created humanity, He created us in His image and likeness. We are created to be like God and to represent God (chapter 3).[46] God gave us something that Satan wanted. Further, God then shared His dominion over creation with us. We were created to rule and reign with Him (Genesis 1:26-28). Again, God gave us something Satan sought. Add the fact that humanity is the very crown of God's creative work, and Satan

---

46 Grudem, *Theology*, 442-443.

surmised that the best way to get back at God was to destroy the beloved "apple of His eye" (Psalm 17:8-9). Not only that, but if Satan could convince us to give up our shared dominion, he could usurp it from us and rule the earth. That's exactly what happened. Now he patrols the earth (Job 1:6-7). He *prowls around like a roaring lion* (1 Peter 5:8). Paul calls him the *god of this world* (2 Corinthians 4:4), and says that he commands the disobedient (Ephesians 2:2). John says he has power over the whole earth (1 John 5:19). Jesus calls him the ruler of this world (John 12:31-32; 14:30; 16:11). And while Jesus decimated Satan's dominion on the cross (1 John 3:8), the battle of the two kingdoms will continue to rage until Christ returns in power and glory. We are inescapably caught up in it.

Ken Boa explains that every human being faces this battle on three fronts: the flesh, the world, and the devil (with his demons).[47] As we seek our Abba to meet our need for protection, these are precisely the areas Jesus taught us to cover with prayer.

Temptation

Jesus teaches us to pray, *Lead us not into temptation.* I admit that this wording has troubled me because the Bible is abundantly clear that God does not tempt anyone. *Let no one say when he is tempted, "I am being tempted by God," for God cannot be tempted with evil, and he himself tempts no one. But each person is tempted*

---

47 Kenneth Boa, *Conformed to His Image: Biblical, Practical Approaches to Spiritual Formation* (Grand Rapids: Zondervan Academic, 2020), 345.

when he is lured and enticed by his own desire. Then desire when it has conceived gives birth to sin, and sin when it is fully grown brings forth death (James 1:13-15).

The Greek word translated as "temptation" here is *peirasmos*, which can also be translated as "trial" or "testing." Some have suggested that a better translation might be, "Do not lead us into testing" or "Do not lead us into tribulation." These are certainly possible. But historically, the idea of temptation has always been associated with Jesus' prayer. So something else must be happening here. God does not tempt, but God does allow us to experience temptation as a form of testing. The very best model for us in this is Jesus Himself (Luke 4:1-13). Thus, the fuller meaning of *peirasmos* is appropriate. James tells us that the problem with temptation is not with God, but with our desires. They are either mastered or they are not, and testing proves them one way or the other. Craig Blomberg writes:

> In light of the probable Aramaic underlying Jesus' prayer, these words seem best taken as "don't let us succumb to temptation" (cf. Mark 14:38) or "don't abandon us to temptation." We do, of course, periodically succumb to temptation, but never because we have no alternative (1 Corinthians 10:13). So when we give in, we have only ourselves to blame.[48]

---

48 Craig L. Blomberg, *Matthew* in *The New American Commentary: An Exegetical and Theological Exposition of Holy Scripture NIV Text* (Nashville: Broadman Press, 1992), 120.

We pray that we will have what we need to endure and ultimately overcome any temptations we face. John Stott concurs: "The probable answer is that the prayer is more that we may overcome temptation, than that we may avoid it. Perhaps we could paraphrase the whole request as 'Do not allow us so to be led into temptation that it overwhelms us, but rescue us from the evil one.'"[49]

We must understand that the influence of the kingdom of darkness is prolific. We may be free from its bondage by the blood of Jesus, but that does not render it fully impotent. There will continue to be power struggles until Jesus returns. The world and our flesh are in partnership against us. Satan has so corrupted the world's systems that, at times, they can hit us like a barrage – and nearly always in areas of our weakness. As we pray for protection in the area of temptation, we must accompany that with the crucifixion of the flesh (and by flesh here, we mean our sinful nature – that part of us that yearns for things that do not honor our Abba). We put our sinful appetites to death, and we ask for help in prayer. This can only be done with the Holy Spirit's help (Romans 8:13).

Paul tells us that if we walk by the Holy Spirit, we will not *gratify the desires of the flesh* (Galatians 5:16). This "walk" is like developing a muscle. It takes time and gets stronger with intentional and graduated practice. We employ spiritual activities (called "spiritual disciplines") such as consistent daily prayer and intercession, Bible reading (and memorization), serving others, worship, thanksgiving, confession (yes, to a confidant

---

[49] Stott, *Message*, 150.

who can help hold us accountable), generosity, discipling others, and more. These help us to partner with the sanctifying work of the Holy Spirit, enabling us to grow stronger in our spiritual walk so that we are less apt to give in to our old nature.

As we pray, we ask our Abba to protect us from our old fleshly appetites. We ask Him to guard our minds, and at the same time, we invite the Holy Spirit to take control. We ask Him to guard our eyes because the world plants things in the most obvious places that we should not see or watch. We ask Him to guard our ears so that we do not listen to the "poison whispers" of those around us. (By the way, these must necessarily include social media, podcasts, talk radio, television, news and information sites, and more!) We ask our Abba to guard our environment so that neither the world nor our enemy can plant corrupting influences right under our noses. We ask the Holy Spirit to show us what things cause us to stumble – to help us identify our triggers – and to enable us by His power to avoid and overcome them. We ask our Abba to protect us from all possible temptations that may be new to us. We ask for protection from the world's influence. And I would add a prayer that our Abba would protect all those we love in the very same ways.

The Evil One

As we beseech our heavenly Father for our protection, there is a second emphasis Jesus instructs us to pursue. He teaches us to pray, *Deliver us from evil* (or the Evil

One). While I believe that most of our challenges with sin in this life are driven by our flesh, there is no doubt that we have a very active enemy working behind the scenes (and sometimes more overtly) to undermine and oppose us as kingdom people. Our destiny is secure in Christ, but this life may still be filled with the oppression, distractions, and direct attacks of the enemy. As we pray to overcome all temptation, we also pray to be delivered from all the plans and activities of Satan and his demons. Jesus knows our weaknesses and our blind spots. Commenting on the two parts of our prayer for protection, R. T. France writes, "The stress in both clauses is on the vulnerability of disciples and their consequent dependence on God for avoiding sin, though the ultimate threat of the eschatological conflict cannot be excluded from the prayer's perspective."[50]

We cannot live in the victory that our Abba intends for us without His help. As with the other stanzas of Jesus' kingdom prayer framework, He teaches us again to call upon the resources and realities of heaven for our protection. Joachim Jeremias explains:

> Jesus has summoned his disciples to ask for the consummation, when God's name will be hallowed and his kingdom come. What is more, he has encouraged them in their petitions to "pray down" the gifts of the age of salvation into their own poor lives, even here and now. But with the soberness which characterizes all his

---

50   France, *Matthew*, 136.

words, Jesus warns his disciples of the danger of false enthusiasm when he calls them abruptly back to the reality of their own threatened existence by means of this concluding petition. This final petition is a cry out of the depths of distress, a resounding call for aid from a man who in affliction prays: "Dear Father, this one request grant us: preserve us from falling away from Thee."[51]

All the protective resources of the kingdom of God, though it is not yet consummated, are at our disposal in this prayer.

Just as our flesh and the world are in an unholy partnership with respect to our temptation, so Satan and his demons are in an alliance for the purposes of oppression and direct spiritual attacks. The demonic realm is real; those who think it is a form of Christian mythology are setting themselves up for peril. When Satan rebelled and was cast out of God's presence in heaven, as many as one-third of the angelic host went with him (Revelation 12:3-4). While Satan and his fallen demonic minions are destined for eternal punishment with no hope of redemption (Matthew 25:41; Revelation 20:10, 14), they are still very active in the cosmic spiritual battle between the kingdoms of light and darkness.

Jesus has won; however, we are in the midst of a "cleanup operation" in this time between Jesus'

---

51 Jeremias, *Prayers*, 106.

incarnation and glorious return. Jesus' kingdom citizens and ambassadors are on His vital redemptive mission to woo more precious souls into the kingdom of God, and Satan will continue to do all that is still within his power to stop us. There is nothing more important than the King and His kingdom rule and reign. Those of us who belong to Him have one primary priority: to make disciples for Jesus.

As we pray, *Deliver us from evil*, we must remember James' instruction:

> *Submit yourselves therefore to God. Resist the devil, and he will flee from you. Draw near to God, and he will draw near to you. Cleanse your hands, you sinners, and purify your hearts, you double-minded. Be wretched and mourn and weep. Let your laughter be turned to mourning and your joy to gloom. Humble yourselves before the Lord, and he will exalt you.* (James 4:7-10)

Many people will say, "Just resist the devil and he will flee from you," but this misses the most important part of James' statement. We must remain in submission to our Abba (that means staying surrendered to His kingdom rule and reign). Only then can we pray and resist, causing the Evil One himself to flee. We pray, "Abba, keep me from the devil and all his plans." We pray, "Abba, help me stand against all demonic oppression, influence, and attack." We pray that we may be able to withstand Satan's strategic use of the world and its lure upon us. And, as with temptation, we also pray for the very same protection for all those we love.

Doxology

Most Christians have been taught to end the disciples' prayer with a doxology: "Thine is the kingdom and the power and the glory forever. Amen." And while this was not part of Jesus' original prayer lesson in Aramaic,[52] it was added by the church very early on. Such a concluding doxology was an essential element in many Jewish prayers.[53] Even this phrasing was common because it was modeled after King David's prayer for the building of the temple:

> *Therefore David blessed the LORD in the presence of all the assembly. And David said: "Blessed are you, O LORD, the God of Israel our father, forever and ever. Yours, O LORD, is the greatness and the power and the glory and the victory and the majesty, for all that is in the heavens and in the earth is yours. Yours is the kingdom, O LORD, and you are exalted as head above all. Both riches and honor come from you, and you rule over all. In your hand are power and might, and in*

---

52 Blomberg, *Matthew*, 120-121. None of the earliest manuscripts of Matthew's gospel contain these words, so it is very unlikely it was original content. However, later manuscripts do include it, so it was not very long before it was added. It is also missing from some of the earliest translations such as the Latin and Coptic versions, as well as in the writings of numerous church fathers.

53 France, *Matthew*, 137.

> *your hand it is to make great and to give*
> *strength to all. And now we thank you,*
> *our God, and praise your glorious name."*
> (1 Chronicles 29:10-13)

It is entirely possible that Jesus used such a doxology at times. The early Christians certainly did. In fact, by the time Jesus' own apostles had coalesced their teaching into a basic first-century catechism (called the *Didache* or *Teaching*), that doxology was already being recited as a regular part of the prayer.[54]

When one understands the beautiful depth and the spiritual importance of Jesus' kingdom prayer framework, there is indeed great reason for praise.[55] This doxology has three critical affirmations:

1. *Yours is the kingdom.* We've spent much time already defining the kingdom of God. This is a public declaration of our Abba's right to rule. As many Jewish prayers begin with the words, "Blessed are you, O Lord, our God, King of the universe," we recognize that His dominion over all creation is nonnegotiable. Once again, there is nothing more important than our King and His kingdom!

2. *Yours is the power.* Remember from our study of our Abba's name that He is the Almighty.

---

54 *The Didache (The Teaching of the Twelve Apostles)*, in *The Apostolic Fathers*, trans. J. B. Lightfoot and J. R. Harmer, ed. Michael W Holmes (Grand Rapids: Baker Book House, 1989), 153.

55 The word "doxology" is from the Greek word *doxa*, which essentially means "giving God glory or praise."

There is nothing our God cannot do. With only a word, He creates. All power and all authority belong to Him!

3. *Yours is the glory.* The glory of God is our Abba's manifest beauty. Our Abba is preeminently magnificent, full of divine splendor, of greatest worth; it is His character, His person. There is no one – no god – greater than our loving Abba!

Because the kingdom of God is here, even though it has yet to come in its fullness, these three affirmations are already true! Our Abba's kingdom is here now. His power is here now. His glory is here now. And because the consummation of His kingdom is coming soon, these are true for all eternity: "forever. Amen!"

The prayer that begins by calling us to recognize our "Abba in the heavens" can rightly end with such a doxology. This is the God to whom we pray, and we can be confident that this is the God who will answer our prayers! *And this is the confidence that we have toward him, that if we ask anything according to his will he hears us. And if we know that he hears us in whatever we ask, we know that we have the requests that we have asked of him* (1 John 5:14-15).

Putting It All Into Practice

Every human being is in a cosmic battle, whether they know it or not. Jesus teaches us how to pray for our protection. As you consider what you have learned in this final chapter, ask the Holy Spirit to guide you through the following questions:

1. How aware have you been of the war between the kingdom of God and the kingdom of Satan? What is your understanding of your own involvement? Are you an intentional warrior of heaven or a pawn of the enemy? Why do you say that?

2. How much of Satan's rebellion did you understand before this chapter? What new insights have you gained?

3. Why does Satan hate you so much? What does that have to do with your life as your Abba's child?

4. Why is it important to understand that God never tempts you?

5. How does one "crucify" the flesh? What steps are you taking to do that for yourself? What else do you need to begin?

6. How do we pray for protection from temptation?

7. Why are the attempts of so many Christians to "resist" the devil unsuccessful? Explain this from the Bible.

8. How do we pray for protection from Satan and his demonic host?

9. Why is the doxology, "Yours is the kingdom

and the power and the glory forever. Amen," a good way to conclude our prayer, even though it was not part of Jesus' original lesson?

10. How can you thank your Abba for everything in this prayer? How can you praise Him for all He does for you?

11. Do you regularly praise your Abba that He rules and reigns forever? Do you praise Him that He is the one who has the ultimate power and authority forever? Do you praise Him for His eternal manifest beauty?

Pause and consider how Jesus has us pray for our three ongoing needs: provision, forgiveness, and protection. What has the Holy Spirit been showing you about your own perspective on these three needs? How might you become more purposeful and consistent in seeking these from your Abba's kingdom resources? If you have been keeping a journal, spend some time processing your answers to all of these questions.

Epilogue

Praying with Kingdom Power

> The enemy will try to limit your praying
> because he knows your praying will limit him.
> —Rick Warren

Many people want to see consistent answers to their prayers. They want to pray with authentic kingdom power, but they are unwilling to become full partners in Jesus' redemptive work. It is impossible to have one without the other. To think we can rattle off a list of our petitions without faithfully engaging in the actual mission of our Abba's kingdom is arrogance. He does not work for us; it's the other way around.

I hope this text on the disciples' prayer has been helpful to you, but please understand that it will be useless to you without first meeting some requirements:

1. **You must be born again.** Sin keeps God from hearing and responding to our prayers

(Psalm 66:18; Proverbs 15:29; Isaiah 1:15; 59:2; Micah 3:4; John 9:31; 1 Peter 3:12). Praying without surrender to God's rule and reign through Jesus Christ is an utterly fruitless exercise. It is true that the first prayer our loving Abba will hear is a person's authentic cry for forgiveness and salvation. You will recall from chapter 1 that for several hundred years, the early church did not even teach the disciples' prayer to people until they had confessed faith in Christ, were converted, and were subsequently baptized. Salvation is still mandatory.

2. **You must be filled with the Holy Spirit.** Kingdom power comes by the presence of our Abba's Spirit. Jesus said, *You will receive power when the Holy Spirit has come upon you, and you will be my witnesses in Jerusalem and in all Judea and Samaria, and to the end of the earth* (Acts 1:8). It is the Holy Spirit who leads us into all truth (John 16:13). It is the Holy Spirit who sets us apart as holy (Romans 1:4). It is the Holy Spirit who gives us new life in Christ (John 6:63), giving us full rights as our loving Abba's adopted daughters and sons (John 1:12-13; Romans 8:15; Galatians 4:4-6). It is the Holy Spirit who enables our prayers – especially when we do not know how to pray (Romans 8:26-28).

3. **You must be engaged in the kingdom mission.** Without exception, to be born again in Christ is to be commissioned into His redemptive kingdom mission (Matthew 28:18-20). In Christ, we not only become our Abba's precious, beloved, redeemed daughters and sons, but we actively join the "family business" as Christ's ambassadors (2 Corinthians 5:20). We cannot refuse the mission and still think our prayers will carry kingdom power. It doesn't work like that.

Do you meet the above criteria? If so, then you are enthusiastically invited by the Savior to pray the disciples' prayer. Pray the outline Jesus has given us consistently and persistently, the way He taught it. The early disciples prayed it three times a day: when they woke up in the morning, at noonday, and before going to bed in the evening. Many Christians still uphold similar prayer practices today.[56] However you decide to employ this powerful kingdom prayer framework, may you experience our mighty God working through you every single day.

My prayer is that your prayer life will increase in both frequency and fruitfulness many times over. May our Abba use you mightily for the advancement of His kingdom and His glory!

---

[56] The Daily Office is a wonderful tool for such praying. Online and app versions are available, including the Daily Office Lectionary App by Jim's Computer Programming, based upon the 1979 *Book of Common Prayer*. See your app store or www.jimscomputerprogramming.com.

Appendixes

> The world we build tomorrow is born on
> the prayers we say today.
> —Rabbi Jonathan Sacks

Prayer has always been a vital part of Jewish life. We noted in this book that Jesus' disciples would have prayed at least three times a day: morning, noon, and night. We also mentioned that each rabbi of Jesus' day provided his disciples with a specific prayer framework according to his own yoke. I am including in these appendixes some samples of the prayers Jewish people have historically prayed.

Appendix One

The Shema

The Shema is arguably the most important prayer in Judaism. The name of the prayer is taken from its first word in Hebrew, *Shema*, which means "hear." It is the creed of the Israelites under Moses that set them apart from all the other people groups of Canaan. It declares that their God is *one* (as opposed to the many gods of the polytheistic nations that surrounded them), and calls them to love God with every fiber of their being.

When Jesus was challenged in Matthew 22:34-40 by a legalist who asked, *Which is the great commandment in the Law?* Jesus responded with the Shema. In fact, you can see how Jesus' life and ministry were shaped by it, prioritized by what Christians now call the Great Commandment and the Great Commission. Originally, the Shema was just the declaration from Deuteronomy 6:4-9. But later, the text from Deuteronomy 11:13-21 and Numbers 15:37-41 was added, providing three key passages from the Torah (Law).

Jewish tradition says that the Shema is to be recited twice a day – once during the morning prayers and again during the evening prayers. Traditionally, it is prayed with one's right hand over one's eyes.

The Shema

Hear, O Israel, the Lord is our God, the Lord is One.

Blessed is the name of His glorious kingdom for ever and ever.

You shall love the Lord your God with all your heart and with all your soul and with all your might. Take to heart these instructions with which I charge you this day. Impress them upon your children. Recite them when you stay at home and when you are away, when you lie down and when you get up. Bind them as a sign on your hand and let them serve as a symbol on your forehead, inscribe them on the doorposts of your house and on your gates (Deuteronomy 6:5-9).

If, then, you obey the commandments that I enjoin upon you this day, loving the Lord your God and serving Him with all your heart and soul, I will grant the rain for your land in season, the early rain and the late. You shall gather in your new grain and wine and oil—I will also provide grass in the fields for your cattle—and thus you shall eat your fill. Take care not to be lured away to serve other gods and bow to them. For the Lord's anger will flare up against you,

*and He will shut up the skies so that there will be
no rain and the ground will not yield its produce;
and you will soon perish from the good land that
the* Lord *is assigning to you. Therefore impress
these My words upon your very heart: bind them
as a sign on your hand and let them serve as a
symbol on your forehead, and teach them to your
children—reciting them when you stay at home
and when you are away, when you lie down and
when you get up; and inscribe them on the doorposts of your house and on your gates—to the
end that you and your children may endure, in
the land that the* Lord *swore to your fathers to
assign to them, as long as there is a heaven over
the earth* (Deuteronomy 11:13-21).

The Lord *said to Moses as follows: Speak to
the Israelite people and instruct them to make
for themselves fringes on the corners of their
garments throughout the ages; let them attach
a cord of blue to the fringe at each corner. That
shall be your fringe; look at it and recall all
the commandments of the* Lord *and observe
them, so that you do not follow your heart and
eyes in your lustful urge. Thus you shall be
reminded to observe all My commandments
and to be holy to your God. I the* Lord *am
your God, who brought you out of the land of
Egypt to be your God: I, the* Lord *your God*
(Numbers 15:37-41).

Appendix Two

The Kiddush

The Kiddush is a special Jewish blessing that is used to sanctify (set apart) the Sabbath and special festivals. It is said over a raised glass of wine before the evening meal and marks the beginning of the weekly Shabbat (Sabbath) or a festival.

The Kiddush recognizes God's creation and the holiness of the seventh day, the Sabbath.

The Kiddush

And there was evening and there was morning, the sixth day.

The heaven and the earth were finished, and all their array. On the seventh day God finished the work that God had been doing, and God ceased on the seventh day from all the work that God had done. And God blessed the seventh day and declared it holy, because on it God ceased from all the work of creation that God had done.

Appendix Three

The Amidah

The Amidah (also called *Shemonah Esreh* ["the Eighteen"] and *HaTefillah* ["the prayer"]) is a central prayer in Jewish tradition. The name comes from the Hebrew word *amidah* (which means "standing") because it is prayed standing up facing Jerusalem, praying quietly to oneself with one's feet together. The prayer is used for daily worship and special services.

"The Eighteen" refers to the eighteen blessings constituting its text. Later, a nineteenth was added.[57] It is prayed three times a day: morning, noon, and evening. Originating in the fifth century BC, it is almost assured that Jesus and His disciples would have been reared praying some form of it. The prayer was standardized in the second century AD and has remained relatively the same since, with certain variations as practiced by various Jewish sects, and alterations for different

---

[57] The twelfth blessing (or benediction) regarding apostates was added around AD 70. This extended the "Eighteen Benedictions" to nineteen.

celebrations and seasons of the year. It is divided into three basic parts: praise, petitions, and thanksgiving.

Because of some similarities, some Bible scholars believe that Jesus may have used it as one of the models for the disciples' prayer. The Amidah may have been on the mind of the unnamed disciple who asked Jesus to teach them to pray (Luke 11:1). References in the Bible about going to the temple at the time of prayer are references to praying the Amidah (e.g., Acts 3:1).

While no Christian groups officially use it for worship, many believers use it in their personal prayer times.

The Amidah

Blessings of Praise

1. ***Avot (Fathers) or The God of History:*** [58]
   Blessed are you, O Lord our God and God of our fathers, the God of Abraham, the God of Isaac, and the God of Jacob, the great, mighty and revered God, the Most High God who bestows loving-kindnesses, the creator of all things, who remembers the good deeds of the patriarchs and in love came as a redeemer to their children's children for your name's sake. O king, helper, savior, and shield. Blessed are you, O Lord, the shield of Abraham.

2. ***Gevurot (God's Might) or The God of Nature:***
   You, O Lord, are mighty forever, you revive the dead, you have the power to save. You cause the wind to blow and the rain to fall.[59] *You sustain the living with loving-kindness, you revive the dead with great mercy, and you support the falling, heal the sick, set free the bound, and keep faith with those who sleep in the dust. Who is like you, O doer of mighty acts? Who resembles you, a king who puts to death and restores to life, and causes salvation to flourish? And you*

---

[58] There are many variations of the Amidah, utilizing different but similar titles for each benediction. I show the two most common titles used today.

[59] This sentence is added from the end of Succoth until the eve of Passover.

are certain to revive the dead. Blessed are you, O Lord, who revives the dead.

3. **Kedushat Hashem (Holiness of God's Name) or The Sanctification of God:** *We will sanctify your name in this world just as it is sanctified in the highest heavens, as it is written by your prophet: And they call out to one another and say: Holy, holy, holy is the Lord of hosts; the whole earth is full of his glory. Blessed be the Presence of the Lord in his place. And in your Holy Words it is written, saying, The Lord reigns forever, your God, O Zion, throughout all generations. Hallelujah. Throughout all generations, we will declare your greatness, and to all eternity we will proclaim your holiness. Your praise, our God, shall never depart from our mouth, for you are a great and holy God and King. Blessed are you, O Lord, the holy God. You are holy, and your name is holy, and holy beings praise you daily. Blessed are you, O Lord, the holy God.*

Blessings of Petition

1. ***Da'at (Knowledge) or For Understanding:*** *You favor men with knowledge, and teach mortals understanding. Oh, favor us with the knowledge, the understanding, and the insight that comes from you. Blessed are you, O Lord, the gracious giver of knowledge.*

2. ***Teshuvah (Repentance) or For Repentance:*** *Bring us back, our Father, to your Instruction; draw us near, our King, to your service; and cause us to return to you in perfect repentance. Blessed are you, O Lord, who delights in repentance.*

3. ***Selichah (Forgiveness) or For Forgiveness:*** *Forgive us, our Father, for we have sinned; pardon us, our King, for we have transgressed; for you pardon and forgive. Blessed are you, O Lord, who is merciful and always ready to forgive.*

4. ***Geulah (Redemption) or For Deliverance from Affliction:*** *Look upon our affliction and plead our cause, and redeem us speedily for your name's sake, for you are a mighty redeemer. Blessed are you, O Lord, the redeemer of Israel.*

5. ***Refuah (Healing) or For Healing:*** *Heal us, O Lord, and we will be healed; save us, and we will be saved, for you are our praise. Oh, grant a perfect healing to all our ailments, for you, almighty King, are a faithful and merciful*

healer. Blessed are you, O Lord, the healer of the sick of his people Israel.

6. **Birkat Hashanim (Prosperity) or For Deliverance from Want:** *Bless this year for us, O Lord our God, together with all the varieties of its produce, for our welfare. Bestow dew and rain for a blessing upon the face of the earth. Oh, satisfy us with your goodness, and bless our year like the best of years. Blessed are you, O Lord, who blesses the years.*

7. **Kibbutz Galuyot (Ingathering of Exiles) or For Gathering of Exiles:** *Sound the great shofar[60] for our freedom, raise the ensign to gather our exiles, and gather us from the four corners of the earth. Blessed are you, O Lord, who gathers the dispersed of your people Israel.*

8. **Birkat Hadin (Restoration of Justice) or For the Righteous Reign of God:** *Restore our judges as in former times, and our counselors as at the beginning; and remove from us sorrow and sighing. Reign over us, you alone, O Lord, with loving-kindness and compassion, and clear us in judgment. Blessed are you, O Lord, the King who loves righteousness and justice.*

9. **Birkat Haminim (Against Heretics) or For the Destruction of Apostates and the Enemies of God:** *Let there be no hope for slanderers, and let all the wickedness perish in an instant. May*

---

60   A shofar is a ram's horn.

all your enemies quickly be cut down, and may you soon in our day uproot, crush, cast down, and humble the dominion of arrogance. Blessed are you, O Lord, who smashes enemies and humbles the arrogant.

10. **Tzaddikim (Righteous Ones) or For the Righteous and Proselytes:** *May your compassion be stirred, O Lord our God, toward the righteous, the pious, the elders of your people, the house of Israel, the remnant of their scholars, toward proselytes, and toward us also. Grant a good reward to all who truly trust in your name. Set our lot with them forever so that we may never be put to shame, for we have put our trust in you. Blessed are you, O Lord, the support and stay of the righteous.*

11. **Binyan Yershalayim (Rebuilding of Jerusalem) or For the Rebuilding of Jerusalem:** *Return in mercy to Jerusalem, your city, and dwell in it as you have promised. Rebuild it soon in our day as an eternal structure, and quickly set up in it the throne of David. Blessed are you, O Lord, who rebuilds Jerusalem.*

12. **Malkhut beit David (Kingdom of David) or For the Messianic King:** *Speedily bring the offspring of your servant David to us, and let him be exalted by your saving power, for we wait all day long for your salvation. Blessed are you, O Lord, who brings salvation to flourish.*

13. ***Kabbalat Tefillah (Acceptance of Prayer) or For the Answering of Prayer:*** *Hear our voice, O Lord our God; spare us and have pity on us. Accept our prayer in mercy and with favor, for you are a God who hears prayers and supplications. Our King, do not turn us away from your presence empty-handed, for you hear the prayers of your people Israel with compassion. Blessed are you, O Lord, who hears prayer.*

Blessings of Thanksgiving

1. ***Avodah (Worship) or For Restoration of Temple Service:*** *Be pleased, O Lord our God, with your people Israel and with their prayers. Restore the service to the inner sanctuary of your Temple, and receive in love and with favor both the fire-offerings of Israel and their prayers. May the worship of your people, Israel, always be acceptable to you. And let our eyes behold your return in mercy to Zion. Blessed are you, O Lord, who restores your divine presence to Zion.*

2. **Hodah'ah (Gratitude) or Thanksgiving for God's Unfailing Mercies:** *We give thanks to you that you are the Lord our God and the God of our fathers forever and ever. Through every generation, you have been the rock of our lives, the shield of our salvation. We will give you thanks and declare your praise for our lives that are committed into your hands, for our souls that are entrusted to you, for your miracles that are daily with us, and for your wonders and your benefits that are with us at all times, evening, morning, and noon. O beneficent one, your mercies never fail; O merciful one, your loving-kindnesses never cease. We have always put our hope in you. For all these acts may your name be blessed and exalted continually, our King, forever and ever. Let every living thing give thanks to you and praise your name in truth, O God, our salvation and our help. Blessed are*

you, O Lord, whose Name is the Beneficent One, and to whom it is fitting to give thanks.

3. **Sim Shalom (Grand Peace) or For Peace:** *Grant peace, welfare, blessing, grace, loving-kindness, and mercy to us and to all Israel, your people. Bless us, our Father, one and all, with the light of your countenance; for by the light of your countenance you have given us, O Lord our God, a Torah of life, loving-kindness and salvation, blessing, mercy, life, and peace. May it please you to bless your people Israel at all times and in every hour with your peace. Blessed are you, O Lord, who blesses his people Israel with peace.*

About the Author

John Kimball, DMin, is the lead pastor of Palmwood Church in Oviedo, Florida. The church has a beautiful partnership with the YMCA of Central Florida, and ministers within the Oviedo YMCA, where John serves as chaplain. John is also Director of Church Development for the Conservative Congregational Christian Conference (www.ccccusa.com) and is a trainer, coach, and consultant with the Praxis Center for Church Development (www.praxiscenter.org). John and his wife, Kathryn, have ministered together for more than thirty-five years and love living in central Florida.

www.ingramcontent.com/pod-product-compliance
Lightning Source LLC
Chambersburg PA
CBHW070142080526
44586CB00015B/1805